BUSINESS ORGANIZATION *and* ENVIRONMENT

BUSINESS ORGANIZATION *and* ENVIRONMENT

B.G. Satyaprasad
Professor and Director
GT Institute of Management Studies and Research
Bangalore

K. Nirmala
Professor of Commerce
Bangalore University

D.S. Gopalakrishna
Dean
GT Institute of Management Studies and Research
Bangalore

Vedananda Murthy
Professor of Commerce
SLN College
Bangalore

I.K. International Publishing House Pvt. Ltd.

NEW DELHI • BANGALORE

Published by
I.K. International Publishing House Pvt. Ltd.
S-25, Green Park Extension
Uphaar Cinema Market
New Delhi–110 016 (India)
E-mail: info@ikinternational.com
Website: www.ikbooks.com

ISBN 978-93-82332-04-6

Published by Krishan Makhijani for I.K. International Publishing House Pvt. Ltd., S-25, Green Park Extension, Uphaar Cinema Market, New Delhi–110 016 and Printed by Rekha Printers Pvt. Ltd., Okhla Industrial Area, Phase II, New Delhi–110 020.

FOREWORD

The subject of Business Organization and Environment has acquired an important status in the field of business studies at the under-graduate level. It embraces the study of the methods, techniques and practices of efficient organizations and management of business.

Till the year 1992, India practiced conservative economic policies and later adopted liberalization, privatization and globalization policies. As a result of this, India witnessed unprecedented economic growth. Huge employment opportunities were created in IT, Construction, Infrastructure, Aviation, Business Process Management and so on. To cater these employment opportunities new academic programmes were started by Universities. BBM is one such programme which equips students with management perspective at under-graduate level. Today, BBM has become preferred programme among the students who wants to be successful in their career.

In the era of ever changing business environment the student must keep his knowledge updated on a continuous basis. From this academic year onwards Bangalore University has updated its syllabus to meet the needs of the contemporary business environment.

Business Organisation and Environment has been written keeping in mind the latest syllabus and also the practical aspects of business. The book includes various aspectus of busines, different forms of business organisation, details of the environment in which a business organisation operates, role of government in business and so on.

The subject of Business Organization and Environment is very vast and exhusative. Authors of this book have attempted to give a brief and specific information as per the requirements of the university syllabus. Appropriate examples have been used to drive the message the student. Special attention is being given to use simple language so that it is easy to understand.

It is the question of pride and delight for me because the authors belong to G.T. Group of Institutions, Bangalore, who are highly qualified and experienced. They have done excellent work to bring out this book and I hope the students will make the best use of this book.

S. T. Anand
Chairman
G.T. Group of Institutions
G.T. Industrial Enterprises
G.T. Cinemas Pvt Ltd
G.T. Mall and Multiplex

PREFACE

Every truth has four corners, as a teacher I give you one corner and it is for you to find the other three.
—Confucius.

Business Organisation and Environment reflects the ever changing and dynamic business world. The year 1991 is a landmark year in the history of Indian economy which stands tall in the backdrop and has given impetus to a strong business world. The robust Indian economy is witnessing turbulent changes ever since and more so post-2001.

This book has been necessitated by the constant growth of the subject matter, as a result of changes in global corporate business space. The ways businesses are conducted these days is currently undergoing a process of diversification and have even broken the geographical boundaries, which no more exist. The economic reforms seen in the different sectors are both a challenge and an opportunity.

After a thorough research process, the authors have come out with a blend and balance of theoretical concepts, techniques and indigenous illustrations from all the areas that might be of relevance to the readers the text is simple, interesting and yet powerful to the students community.

The authors have also summarized each chapter at the end of each chapter, which can definitely come handy to the lecturers and students in the last minute preparation for the examinations.

The authors sincerely thank the work done by Prof. Anupama and Prof. S. Sathyeshwar for their valuable contribution in bringing out this book.

Lastly, the authors will welcome any suggestions for improving further editions. Readers can write to *info.gteducation@gmail.com* with their valuable feedback.

Wish you all good luck and success in your endeavours.

Authors

CONTENTS

AUTHORS

B.G. Satyaprasad M.Com, MBA, Ph.D

B.G. Satyaprasad, 'finance guru' as his students fondly call him, is an outstanding academician of repute who is also decorated with 'Best Teacher' award (2003) by the Govt. of Karnataka for the exceptional services rendered by him in the field of commerce and management education. A prolific writer who has authored over twenty-five books in the area of commerce and management. He has also guided several M.Phil and Ph.D scholars. He is guiding several educational institutions in India to achieve excellence in the quality of education. He is a consultant for accreditation and quality certifications such as NAAC, NBA, and ISO etc. He is an expert in establishing institutions for higher education. He is also known as an authority on distance learning programme. He has designed and established distance education programmes for several universities. He has served many committees of UGC and other leading universities in enhancing the quality of higher education. Currently he is serving as Director at GT Group of Institutions, Bangalore.

K. Nirmala M.Com, MBA, PhD

A researcher and a seasoned academician having over two decades of teaching experience in commerce.

Currently serving as a member of faculty in the Department of Business Studies, Bangalore University. She has been awarded a Doctorate in Finance by Bangalore University.

She has guided two Ph.D scholars and several M.Phil scholars.

She has presented and chaired several state, national and international conferences.

D.S. Gopalakrishna MA, MBA, MPhil, PhD

An avid researcher having ten years of corporate experience and seven years of academic experience. Currently serving as Dean at GT Group of Institutions, Bangalore. He has been awarded a doctorate in Economics by VMU, for his research on Industrial Economics. He has contributed many articles in various national level journals and newspapers. He has coauthored many books in the area of Services Marketing, Entrepreneurship and Business Communications.

Vedananda Murthy M.Com, EMBA, Ph.D

One of the seniormost teachers in the area of commerce having over 3 decades of experience in academics. Currently serving as a Professor of Commerce in SLN First Grade College, Bangalore.

He has participated, presented research papers in many state & national level conferences.

He has been awarded a Doctorate by Bangalore University in Finance for his research work on 'Asset Liability Management of Commercial Banks'.

Unit 1

Business Organization and Environment

Meaning of Business – Nature of business – Meaning of Profession – Difference between business and profession – Characteristic features of business – Classification of business activities – Trade – Aids of trade – Importance of business – Objectives of business – Goals – Vision – Mission of business – Classification of industries - Secondary industries – Importance of commerce – Advantages and disadvantages of trade and aids to trade.

LEARNING OBJECTIVES

This chapter takes the reader to the basic concepts of business – commerce – trade and aids to trade. This would conceptualize the idea of carrying out a business. It is elementary in nature, even a common should be familiar with the business.

MEANING OF BUSINESS

- "A business may be defined as an institution organized and operated to provide goods and services to the society with the objective of earning profit". L.R. Dikson has defined business as a form of activity pursued primarily with the object of earning profit for the benefit of those on whose behalf the activity is conducted. Business involves production and/or exchange of goods and services to earn profit or in a broader sense, to earn a living, profit is not the sole objective of the business. It may have other objectives like promotion of welfare of the workers and the general public. Business activities include production and distribution of goods and services which satisfy human wants.

1

Business Organization and Environment

The term business should always be used to provide the same meaning as the term trade where it denotes purchase and sale of goods. Business includes all activities from production to distribution of goods and services. It embraces industry, trade, and other activities like banking, transport, insurance and warehousing which facilitate production and distribution of goods and services. According to F.C. Hopper "The whole complex field of commerce and industry which includes the basic industries, processing and manufacturing industries, and the network of ancillary services; distribution, banking, insurance, transport, and so on, which serve and interpenetrate the world of business as a whole" are called business activities.

NATURE OF BUSINESS

The basic cause of all productive activities is the unlimited wants of human beings and the need to satisfy them. Human wants are many and also complex in nature. Though the basic requirements of human beings are food, clothing and shelter, but we are not satisfied with them alone. We consume or use many other things which have to be generally paid for. Each one of them has a long process behind it.

Take, for example, a toilet soap. It is manufactured or produced by a company say, Tata Oil Mills Limited or Hindustan Lever Limited. They procure oils, fats, etc. which are the basic raw materials used in the soap. These raw materials are processed into soap cakes with the help of men and machines. Then these cakes are packed or wrapped in attractive printed paper. Though the soap is ready, it is not available to you at this stage, because it is still in the factory. The soaps are

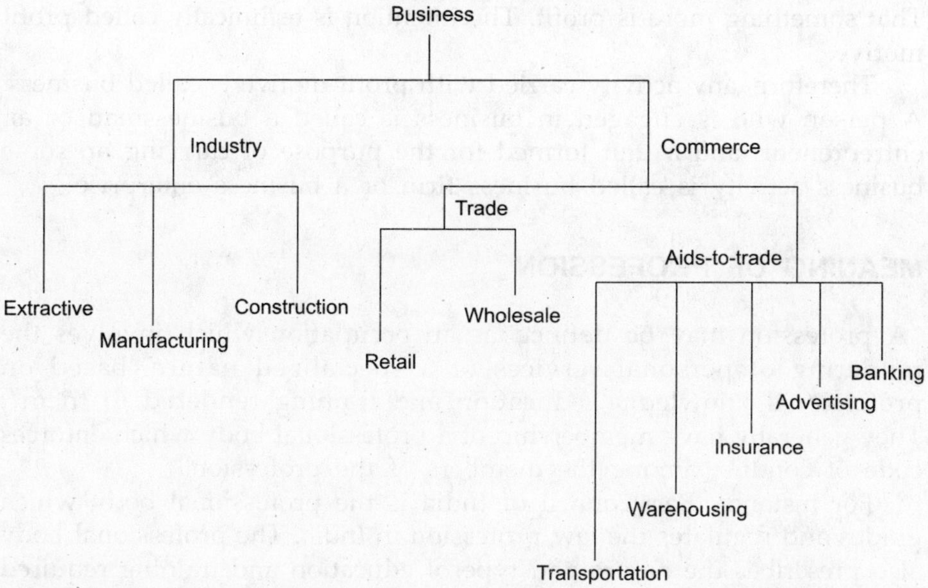

shifted from the factory and stored in company's warehouse. The producer sells the soap to wholesalers who buy it in large quantities and move it to various places and keep them in their warehouses. The wholesale trader, in turn, sells in smaller quantities to the retail traders. The shop in your locality, from which you purchase your soap, is one such retail outlet. In simple terms, this is the story of your soap reaching you. The manufacturer produces goods for the consumer. Sometimes there may not be anybody between the two, but often the manufacturer may take the help of middlemen like the wholesalers and retailers to distribute the goods to consumers. The chart below shows the flow of goods from the time of manufacturing to the ultimate consumers:

Flow of Goods

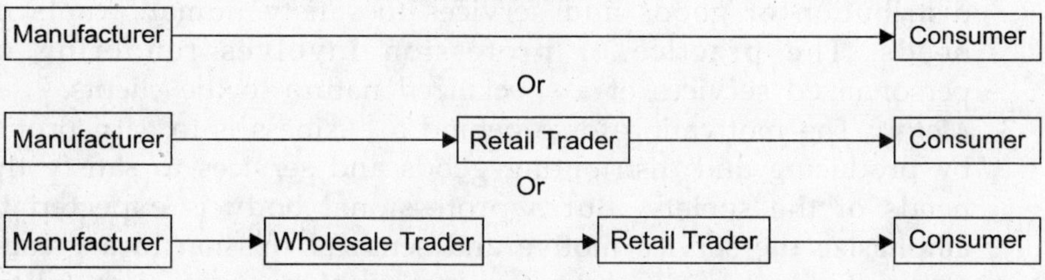

Certain other agencies like banks, insurance companies, transportation firms, warehouses, advertising agencies, etc. also aid the functioning of manufacturers and traders. The intention is to earn something more than what they spend in carrying out the activity.

That something more is profit. The intention is technically called profit motive.

Therefore, any activity carried with profit motive is called business. A person who is engaged in business is called a businessman or an entrepreneur, and a unit formed for the purpose of carrying on some business activity is called business firm or a business enterprise.

MEANING OF PROFESSION

"A profession may be defined as an occupation which involves the rendering of personal services of a specialized nature, based on professional knowledge, education and training rendered to them". They generally have membership of a professional body which enforces code of conduct among the members of the profession.

For instance, Bar Council of India is the professional body which guides and regulates the law profession in India. The professional body also prescribes the nature and type of education and training required to practise the concerned profession.

Distinction between Business and Profession

The terms business and profession are similar in many aspects. But they also differ from each other as stated below:

1. *Establishment:* A business enterprise comes into existence when an entrepreneur takes a decision to carry on production and/or exchange of goods and services in order to earn profits by satisfying the needs of the customers.

   On the other hand, a professional firm is established by the professional (lawyer, chartered accountant, architect, etc.) who holds the membership and the certificate of practice of the concerned professional body.
2. *Nature of Operations:* A business is engaged in the production and distribution of goods and services to satisfy human wants or needs. The practice of profession involves rendering of personalized services of a specialized nature to the clients.
3. *Motive:* The motivating force behind a business is to earn profits by producing and distributing goods and services to satisfy the needs of the society. But a professional body is expected to emphasize the service motive and sense of mission to a greater extent than a businessman. A professional is expected to follow a code of conduct on ethical behaviour specially provided for the profession.
4. *Qualifications:* No qualification is prescribed by any authority for a businessman. In case of profession, specialized knowledge and training are compulsory.

5. *Investment:* Almost every business needs some capital. The amount of capital required varies from business to business and it also depends upon the scale of operations. A professional also has to invest some money to establish an office for rendering professional services.
6. *Reward:* A businessman earns profit, a professional earns fee and an employee earns salary.
7. *Transferability of Interest:* Transfer of ownership is possible in case of business by following the prescribed formalities. It is not possible to transfer ownership interest in case of a profession or employment.

Nature of Business or Characteristics of Business

A business enterprise has the following characteristics.

1. *Dealing in Goods and Services:* Goods produced or exchanged may be consumer goods such as bread, rice, cloth, etc. or capital goods such as machines, tools, etc. The consumer goods are meant for direct consumption either immediately or after undergoing some processes, whereas the capital goods are meant for being used for the purpose of further production. Capital goods are also known as producer's goods. Services include supply of electricity, gas, water, finance, insurance, transportation, warehousing, etc.
2. *Production and Exchange:* Every business is concerned with production and exchange of goods and services for value (price). Thus, goods produced or purchased for personal consumption or for presenting to others as gifts do not constitute business because there is no sale or transfer for value involved. If, for example, 'x' buys a T.V. in Tokyo to be gifted to his brother on

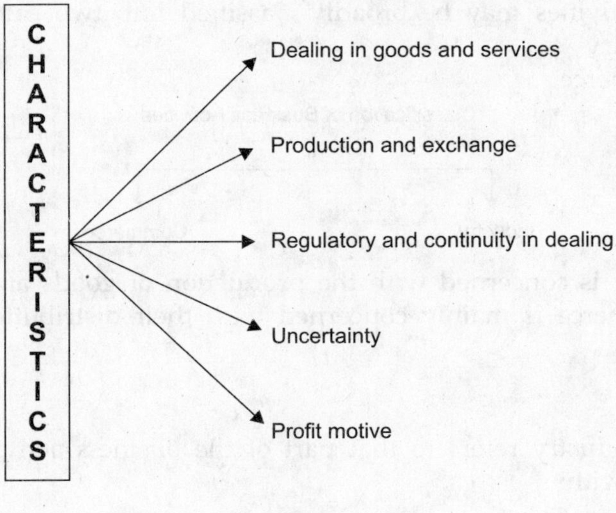

his return to New Delhi, it will not amount to business. But if the same person realizes the price of T.V. set, it will come under the scope of business in a limited way provided the other conditions are also satisfied.

3. *Regularity and Continuity in Dealings:* One sale transaction cannot strictly constitute a business. A sale of a product can be called business if it is undertaken frequently. If other essential characteristics of business are present and the production of goods or rendering of services for a price is undertaken regularly and continuously, this activity will be called business.
4. *Uncertainty or Risk:* Business activities carry an element of risk or uncertainty. It is true that the risk is present in almost all economic activities in a small or great measure. But it is certainly more significantly present in business activities. Risk involves the possibility of loss or what may be called uncertainty of return on investment made in the business due to variety of factors over which the business enterprise has practically little or no control.
5. *Profit Motive:* Human beings are engaged in business primarily to earn profits and acquire wealth. This in no way reduces the importance of service motive in business. As a matter of fact, there is a positive relationship between proper and satisfactory service to the customers and to the society and the extent of profit. Profit motive is also accepted as a desirable objective even for the government enterprises engaged in business. It is called surplus instead of profit in case of government enterprises.

CLASSIFICATION OF BUSINESS ACTIVITIES

Business activities may be broadly classified into two categories:

(i) Industry
(ii) Commerce

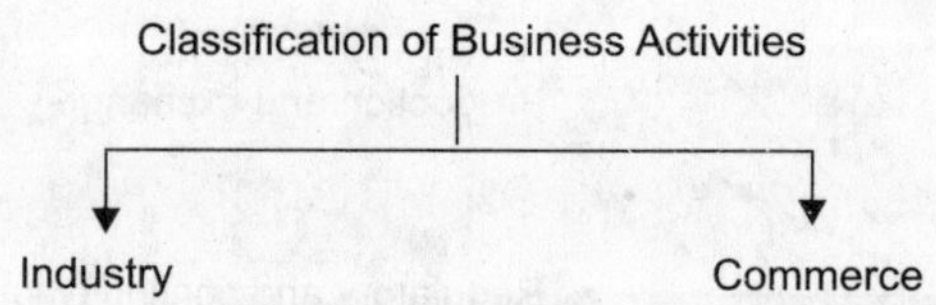

Industry is concerned with the production of goods and materials, while commerce is mainly concerned with their distribution.

Industry

The term industry refers to that part of the business activity which is concerned with:

(a) Extracting materials like coal, iron ore, petroleum (called extractive industry)
(b) Processing and converting raw materials into finished products like soap, bread, fans, machines, cement (called manufacturing industry)
(c) Construction activity like buildings, dams, bridges, roads, etc. (called construction industry)

In other sense, industry means a group of factories usually specializing in a particular product line. For example, all those factories which produce cotton textiles together constitute cotton textile industry.

All the cement factories together constitute cement industry.

Commerce

While industry is concerned with the production of goods, commerce is concerned with making the same available to those who need them. In other words, commerce deals with distribution of goods and services. It includes all those functions which are essential for maintaining a free and uninterrupted flow of goods and services. The term commerce always includes trade and aids-to-trade.

Importance of Business

Business is an integral part of modern society. It is an organized and systematic activity for earning profit. It is concerned with activities of people working towards a common economic goal. Modern society cannot exist without business. The importance of business can be described as follows:

(1) Business improves the standard of living of the people by providing better quality and large variety of goods and services at the right time and at the right place.
(2) It utilizes the scarce resources of the nation and facilitates mass production of goods and services.
(3) It provides opportunities to work and earn a livelihood. Thus, it generates employment in the country, which in turn reduces poverty.
(4) It improves national image by producing and exporting quality goods and services to foreign countries. By participating in international trade fairs and exhibitions it also demonstrates the progress and achievements of its own country to the outside world.
(5) It enables the people of a country to use quality goods of international standard. This is possible by way of importing goods

from foreign countries or by producing quality goods in the country by applying modern methods of production.

(6) It promotes social interest by providing tourist services, sponsoring cultural programmes, trade shows, etc. in the country which enable people of different parts of the country to exchange culture, traditions, and practices. Thus, it promotes national integration.

(7) It also facilitates exchange of culture among the people of different nations and thus, maintains international harmony and peace.

(8) It helps in the development of science and technology. It spends large amount of money on research and development in search of new products and services. Hence, a number of innovative products and services are developed through industrial research.

Objectives of Business

Business objectives are goals which a business organization wants to achieve or accomplish over a specified period of time. It is generally believed that a business has a single objective, that is to make profit and safeguard the interest of its owners. However, no business can ignore the interests of its employees, customers as well as the interest of society as a whole. Business objectives also need to be aimed at contributing to national goals and aspirations as well as towards international well-being. Thus, the objectives of business may be classified as;

(a) Economic objectives
(b) Social objectives
(c) Human objectives
(d) National objectives
(e) Global objectives

Objectives of Business

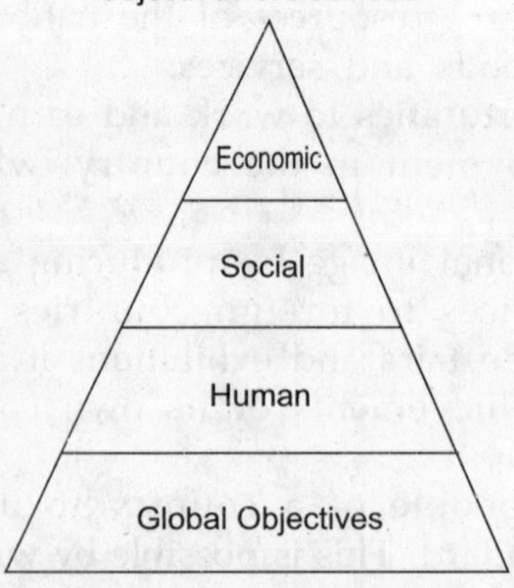

(a) *Economic objectives:* The objectives of earning profit and those which have a different impact in the profit earning objectives of business. Some of the main economic objectives of business are:

(1) Earning adequate profits
(2) Exploring new markets and creation of more customers
(3) Growth and expansion of business operations
(4) Making innovations and improvements in goods and services
(5) Making use of available resources in the best possible manner.

(b) *Social objectives:* These are desired to be achieved for the benefit of the society. Some of the major social objectives are:

(1) Production and supply of quality goods and services to the society.
(2) Making goods available at reasonable prices.
(3) Avoidance of unfair practices like hoarding, black-marketing overcharging, etc.
(4) Contributing towards the general welfare and upliftment of the society.
(5) Ensuring fair return to the investors.
(6) Taking steps in the direction of consumer education.
(7) Conserving natural resources and wildlife and protecting the environment.

(c) *Human objectives:* Primarily refers to the objectives aimed at safeguarding the interest of its employees and their welfare. Some of the major human objectives are:

(1) Providing fair remuneration and incentives to the employees.
(2) Arranging better working conditions and proper work environment for the employees.
(3) Providing job satisfaction by making the jobs interesting and challenging, putting the right person in the right job.
(4) Providing the employees with more and more promotional opportunities.
(5) Organizing training and development programmes for the growth of employees.
(6) Providing employment to the backward classes of the society and people who are physically and mentally challenged.

(d) *National objectives:* The objectives of fulfilling the national goals and aspirations like:

(1) Creation of employment opportunities.
(2) Promotion of social justice.

(3) Produce and supply goods in accordance with the national interest and priorities.

(4) Payment of taxes and other dues honestly and regularly.

(5) Helping the state in maintaining law and order by promoting good industrial relations.

(6) Implementing government's economic and financial policies framed from time to time.

(e) *Global objectives:* Primarily refers to the objectives of facing the challenges of global market. Some of them are as follows:

(1) Making available globally competitive goods and services.

(2) Reducing disparities among rich and poor nations by expanding its operations.

Goals of Business

The terms business goal is used in two senses. Broadly, it refers to the long-term, ultimate purpose of the organization. It is often used to short-term specific targets. The terms vision, mission, objectives, goals and targets are used many a times interchangeably. Mission leads to objectives, objectives lead to goals, and goals lead to targets.

Few typical business goals are:

1. Growth – an organization should grow in terms of market share, sales and profitability
2. Reduce costs
3. Improve customer service and satisfaction
4. Forming relationships with customers and suppliers
5. Improve awareness of IT capabilities within the business
6. Nurture capable manpower to head the business

VISION AND MISSION STATEMENTS OF TOP INDIAN COMPANIES

TATA MOTORS

The vision statement of Tata Motors Limited, India's largest automobile company, is to be "best in the manner in which we operate, best in the products we deliver, and best in our value system and ethics." The mission statement of Passenger Car Business Unit of Tata Motors is:

- To be most admired multi-national Indian car company producing vehicles that people love to buy".
- To create an organization that people enjoy working for, doing business with and investing in".

ADITYA BIRLA GROUP

Vision: To be a premium global conglomerate with a clear focus on each business.

Mission: To deliver superior value to our customers, shareholders, employees and society at large.

GODREJ HERSHEY'S

Vision: Our vision is to be a leader in the Indian food and beverage space by breaking into the exclusive league of top ten FMCG food companies in India.

Mission: Our mission is to do sales of Rs. 1000 crore by 2012, profitably at margins that are best in class in FMCG goods. We will achieve it through unparalleled business innovations and consumer satisfaction.

INFOSYS

Vision: "We will be a globally respected corporation."

Mission: "Strategic Partnerships for Building Tomorrow's Enterprise."

ONGC

Vision: To be a world-class Oil and Gas Company integrated in energy business with dominant Indian leadership and global presence.

INDIAN OIL CORPORATION

Vision: To become a major diversified, transnational, integrated energy company, with national leadership and a strong environment conscience, playing a national role in oil security and public distribution.

VISION

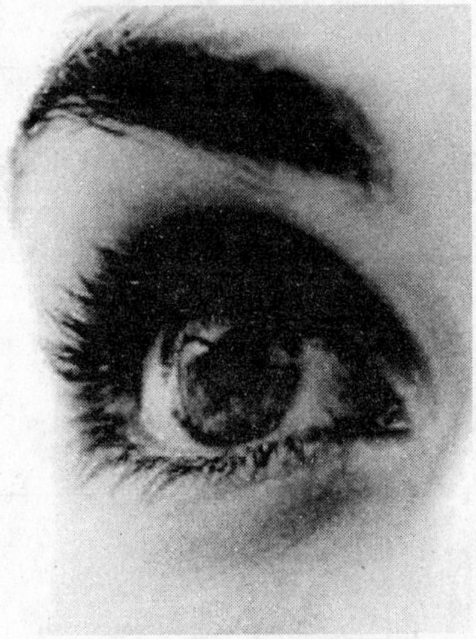

VISION/MISSION

Mission also known as vision, value statement, principles, is the pivot around which corporate strategy revolves. Although mission and vision are often used as synonyms, sometimes a distinction is made in which case mission evolves from the vision. However, sometimes vision and

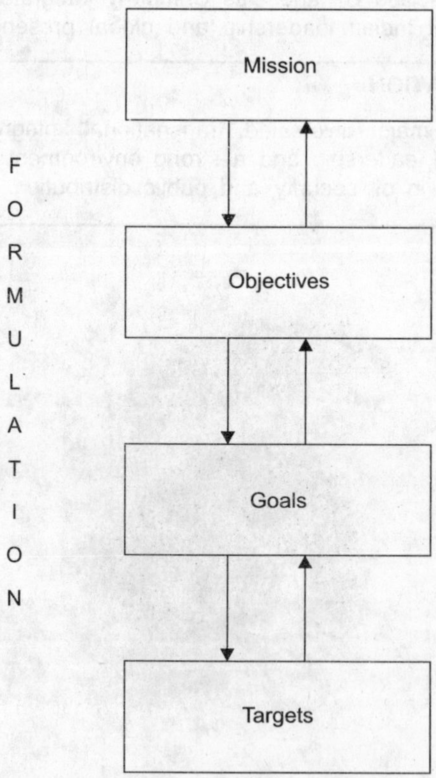

mission are used distinctively and in such cases the vision, i.e., the long-term perception as to what should be the purpose and place of the organization in the future business scenario leads to the mission. Peter Drucker observes that "business purposes and business mission are so rarely given adequate thought is perhaps the most important single cause of business frustration and business failure". He concludes that "defining the purpose and mission of business is difficult, painful, and its resources and got work. It alone enables a business to be managed by performance". "A mission statement is an enduring statement of purpose that distinguishes one business from the similar firms". As Fred David observes, a mission statement reveals the long term vision of an organization in terms of what it wants to be and whom it wants to serve. It describes an organization's purpose, customers, products or services, markets, philosophy, and basic technology. In combination, these components of a mission statement answer a key question about an enterprise. "What is our business?" A good answer to this question makes strategy formulation, strategy implementation and strategy evaluation activities much easier". Mission, objectives, goals and targets–sequence of formulation and achievement.

OBJECTIVES, GOALS AND TARGETS

Objectives form the basis for the functioning of an organization. Indeed "objectives help define the organization in its environment. Most organizations need to justify their existence to legitimize themselves in the eyes of government, customers, and society at large. And by stating objectives, they also attract people who identify with the objectives to work for the organization. Thus, objectives define the enterprise". In other words, objectives may be defined as "the long-term results that an organization seeks to achieve in pursuing its basic mission". Goals are short-term (one year or less) milestones or benchmarks that organizations must achieve in order for long-term objectives to be reached. Goals should be measurable, quantitative, challenging, realistic, consistent and prioritized. They should be established at the corporate, divisional, and functional levels in a large organization. Goals should be stated in terms of management, marketing, finance, production and research and development accomplishments. A set of goals is needed for each objective that is established in organization. Goals are specifically important in strategy implementation, whereas objectives are particularly important in strategy formulation. Goals represent the basis for allocating resources.

Objectives should not be static; they should be dynamic in nature. That is, changes in the environment and/or changes in the organizational strengths and weaknesses may call for modifications to objectives. A company should therefore, appraise how well its objectives tap the firm's opportunities and resources. Dynamic companies often conduct audit of their objectives and reformulate or reorient the objectives, if desirable, to ensure that the company objectives are the most appropriate, given the environment and the company resources. It is such appraisal and the resultant reorientation of the business which enables companies to achieve remarkable success which is often reflected in the prudent portfolio strategies and fast growth of business.

EMPLOYMENT

We have seen people going regularly to offices, factories, firms, etc. for work. These are individuals who are engaged by organizations or individuals to work for them in return for a wage or salary. They are said to be in employment. Thus, we find a postman is in employment in the department of post to deliver letters. Here the department is called the employer and the postman is the employee. The postman works on the basis of certain terms and conditions and gets a monthly salary in return. The main features of employment are:

(1) It is an occupation where a person called employee is to work for another called employer.

(2) There are certain terms and conditions of work like hours of work (how many hours of work a day), duration of work (how many days or hours a week or a month), leave facility, salary/wages, place of work, etc.

(3) The employees get salary (normally paid on monthly basis) or wage (normally paid on daily/weekly basis) in return of their work. This amount is normally predetermined, mutually agreed upon and may increase over time.

(4) Legally the employer-employee relationship is based on a contract and any deviation from any side permits the other party to take legal recourse.

(5) There are jobs for which no technical education or specified skill is required for employment. But for skilled jobs, specialized jobs and technical jobs, a certain level of basic/technical education is required.

(6) The main purpose behind employment is to secure assured income through wages and salaries.

Comparison of Business, Profession and Employment

Having learnt about the essential characteristics, objectives of business, let us distinguish these from profession and employment.

	Basis	Business	Profession	Employment
(1)	Establishment	Decision to start the business and compliance of legal formalities, like registration, wherever required.	Membership of a professional body is essential.	Enter into service contract with the employer.
(2)	Qualification	Specific qualification of is not required.	Professional knowledge and training in the same field is essential.	As per the needs of the employer and job involved.
(3)	Capital	Capital investment is a must and depends on the nature of and scale of business operation.	Some amount of capital investment is required for establishment.	No capital investment is required.
(4)	Nature of work	Production or purchase and sale of goods or services.	Expert services.	Performance of job.
(5)	Return or Reward	Profit	Professional fees	Wages or salary
(6)	Risk	There is no loss.	Risk of not getting sufficient fee.	No risk, so long as business/office continues its operations.
(7)	Motive	Profit motive.	Service motive, though fee is charged.	Motive is to earn a livelihood.

Industry

Industry primarily refers to all such business activities concerned with production/raising or processing of goods and services. It processes raw materials or semi-finished goods into finished goods. Extracting raw materials from earth's surface, manufacturing goods and commodities, producing crops, fish, flowers, etc., constructing buildings, dams, roads, etc. are all example of industry. These activities are called industrial activities and the units engaged in these activities are known as industrial enterprises. However, in a broader sense, provision of services like banking, insurance, transport also form part of industries known as tertiary industries.

CLASSIFICATION OF INDUSTRIES

Before classifying industries on the basis of nature of activity, let us have a broad idea of different approaches of its classification.

	On the basis of nature of activity	*On the basis of nature of goods produced*	*On the basis of level of investment*	*On the basis of size of activity*
(a)	Primary industries	Consumer goods	Heavy industries	Small-scale
(b)	Secondary industries	Produces goods or capital goods	Light industries	Large-scale industries
(c)	Tertiary industries	N.A.	N.A.	N.A.

Primary Industry

Primary industries refer to the activities of natural resources like coal, oil, minerals, etc. and reproduction and development of living organisms like plants and animals, etc. Primary industries can be categorized as extractive and genetic industries. Example, ONGC – It is a company that extracts oil and natural gas from the earth. Similarly, we have farmers growing crops, business houses engaged in extracting raw materials/minerals from the earth (coal mines, iron ore mines, etc.) extracting materials from forest for further processing (like collecting natural honey, timber, etc.), extracting items from sea/river (like fish, crab, prawn, seafood, etc.). All these are examples of extractive industries. Poultry forms, or apple orchards or nurseries are industries engaged in rearing and breeding animals and birds and growing plants or flowers for sale are known as genetic industries. Nowadays genetic industries are growing in numbers which include horticulture, (growing fruits and vegetable), floriculture (growing flowers), dairy farming, poultry farming, pisciculture (breeding fish), etc.

Secondary Industries

The products of primary industries are normally used as raw materials to produce a variety of finished goods. And it is the secondary industry that uses the products of primary industry as its raw materials. The activities of secondary industries may be of manufacturing or construction. Manufacturing industries are engaged in producing finished goods out of raw materials or semi-finished products. For example, cotton is used to produce textile, timber to produce furniture, bauxite to produce alumina. The industries engaged in erection of buildings, dams, bridges, roadways, railways, canals, tunnels, etc. are known as construction industries. They make use of the products of other industries and construct different types of structures as per the requirements of the customer. Manufacturing industry may be divided further into following categories:

(a) Analytical Industries
Manufactures different types of products by analyzing and separating different elements from the same product. Petrol, diesel, kerosene, lubricating oil, etc. are produced from the crude oil in oil refinery industry.

(b) Synthetic Industries
Put together various ingredients and manufacture a new product. For instance, soap is produced by combining potassium carbonate and vegetable oil. Similarly, cement is produced by using limestone, coal, and other chemicals.

(c) Processing Industries
Are those where raw materials are processed through successive stages to get the final products. Textile, sugar and paper are examples of processing industry.

(d) Assembling Industries
Put together various manufactured products and make a new product as in case of car, scooter, bicycle, radio, television, etc.

Tertiary Industry

These industries are basically concerned with generating or processing various services and facilitate the functioning of primary industry and secondary industries as well as activities to trade. These include service industries like, banking, insurance, transport, etc. Film industry which provides entertainment to the individuals, produces films, tourism

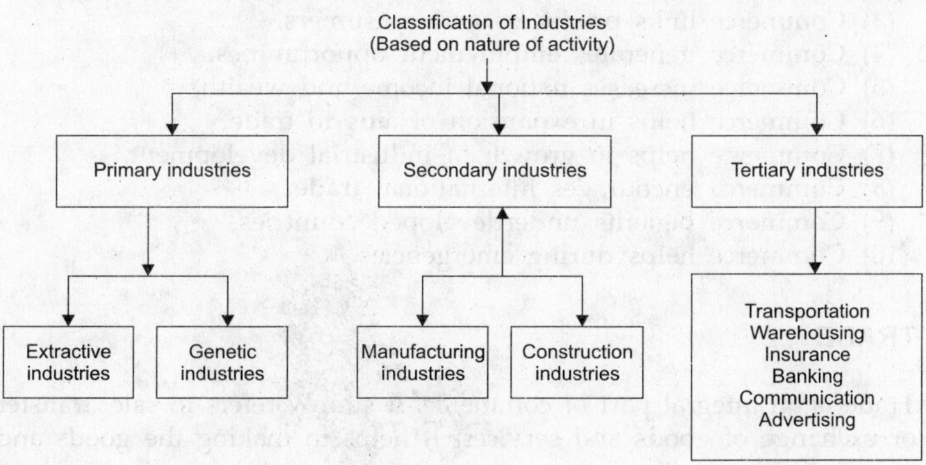

industry which provides services to the individual by facilitating their travel, booking of tickets and hotel rooms, etc. are also included in this category.

COMMERCE

All goods and services are to be made available by those who need them. Commerce is a branch of business. It is concerned with the exchange of goods and services. It includes all activities, which directly on indirectly facilitate that exchange. Commerce looks after the distribution aspect of the business. Whatever is produced it must be consumed, to facilitate this consumption there must be a proper distribution channel. Here comes the need for commerce which is concerned with the smooth buying and selling of services.

Definition of Commerce

According to James Stephenson, "Commerce is an organized system for the exchange of goods between the members of the industrial world". In a broader sense, "Commerce is that part of business which is concerned with the exchange of goods and services and includes all those activities which directly or indirectly facilitate that exchange".

Importance of Commerce

The importance of trade and commerce are mentioned in the following:

(1) Commerce tries to satisfy increasing human wants.
(2) Commerce helps to increase our standard of living.
(3) Commerce links producers and consumers.
(4) Commerce generates employment opportunities.
(5) Commerce increases national income and wealth.
(6) Commerce helps in expansion of aids to trade.
(7) Commerce helps in growth of industrial development.
(8) Commerce encourages international trade.
(9) Commerce benefits underdeveloped countries.
(10) Commerce helps during emergencies.

TRADE

Trade is an integral part of commerce. It simply refers to sale, transfer or exchange of goods and services. It helps in making the goods and services available to ultimate consumers. The manufacturers of goods who produce in bulk or large quantity generally find it very difficult to sell those goods directly to the consumers. The reasons may be distance of the consumers from the place of manufacturing or the quantity of the product bought at one part of time, the problem of payment, and so on. Hence, they utilize the services of some firms or individuals who buy goods from the manufacturers and sell it to the consumers.

For example, the local grocery shop owner sells grocery items to the consumers after buying it from the manufacturers. Sometimes, he buys it from the wholesalers who buy goods in bulk from the manufacturers and sells it to him. It may be noted that the wholesalers as well as the grocery shop owners are said to be engaged in trading. Thus, the features of trade can be summed as follows:

(1) It involves actual buying and selling of goods.
(2) It refers to procuring goods from one place/person to sell it to another person or at another place.
(3) Traders, also known as middlemen facilitate the distribution of goods.
(4) Trading helps, in equalizing demand and supply. For example, the state of Punjab may be producing plenty of rice without much demand for it in its own state. Traders buy rice from Punjab and make it available to states like Orissa and West Bengal where there is great demand for rice. Thus, the demand and supply ratio is maintained.

On the basis of area of operation, trade can be classified as under:

(a) Internal trade
(b) External trade

(a) Internal trade

When trade takes place within the boundaries of a country it is called internal trade. It means both the buying and selling take place within the country. For example, a trader can buy woollen garments from the manufacturers at Ludhiana and sell it to the retailers in Delhi. Similarly, a trader of a village can buy goods from the wholesale market of a city for sale in the village. From these two examples, we find that internal trade can be:

(i) Buying from manufacturers and selling it to retailers in bulk (known as wholesale trade)
(ii) It can be buying from manufacturers or wholesalers and selling it to consumers (known as retail trade)

(b) External trade

Trade that takes place between countries is known as external trade. In other words, external trade refers to buying and/or selling of goods/services across national boundaries. This may take any of the following forms:

(1) Firms of country 'A" purchase goods from firms of country 'B' to be sold in their own country. This is known as import trade.

(2) Firms of country 'A' sells goods produced in their own country to firm of country 'B'. This is known as export trade.

(3) Firms of country 'A' purchase goods from firms of 'B' to be sold to firms of country 'C'. This is known as entrepot trade.

Aids/Auxiliaries Trade

Trade or exchange of goods involves several difficulties, which are removed by auxiliaries known as aids to trade. It refers to all those activities, which directly or indirectly facilitate smooth exchange of goods and services. Aids to trade include transport, communication, warehousing, banking, insurance, advertising, salesmanship, mercantile agents. Auxiliaries ensure smooth flow of goods from producers to consumers.

The various aids to trade in commerce are explained below following:

(1) *Transport:* In the modern times there and vast distances between centres of production and centres of consumption. This difficulty

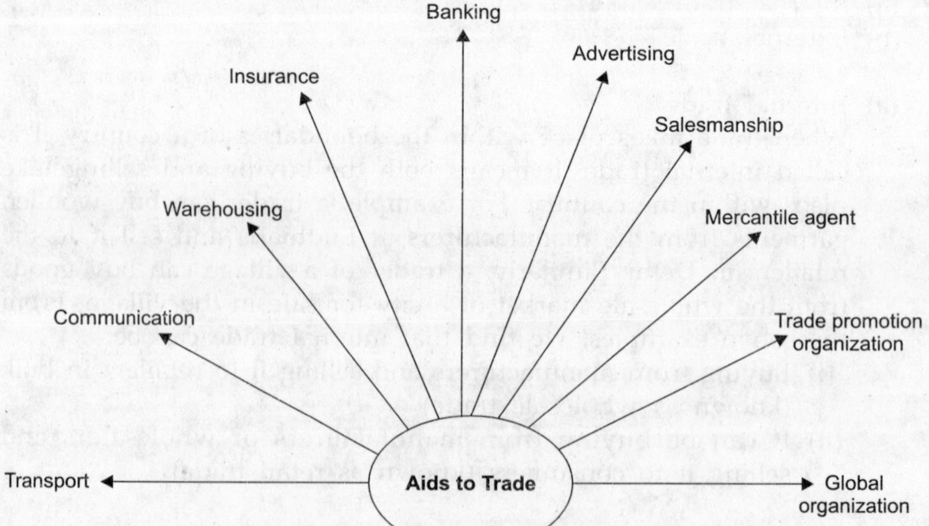

is removed by an important aid to trade known as transport. Transport creates place utility. There are several kinds of transport such as air, water and land transport. The geographical distance between producers and consumers is removed with the help of transport.

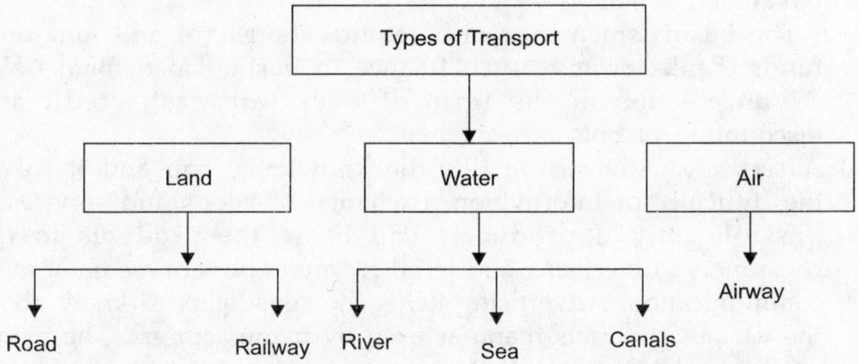

(2) *Communication:* Communication means transmitting or exchange of information from one person to another. It can be oral or written. It is necessary to communicate information from one to another to finalize and settle the terms of sales such as price of goods, discount allowed, facility of credit, etc. Modern means of communication like telephone, telex, fax, telegraph, email, SMS, teleconferencing, videoconferencing, etc. play an important role in establishing contact between businessmen, producers and consumers.

(3) *Warehousing:* There is a time gap between production and consumption. In other words, goods, which are produced at one time, are not consumed at the same time. Hence, it becomes necessary to make arrangements for storage or warehousing. Agricultural commodities like wheat and rice are seasonal in nature but are consumed throughout the year. On the other hand, goods such as umbrellas and woollen sweaters or clothes are produced throughout the year but are demanded only during particular seasons. Therefore, goods need to be stored in the warehouses till they are demanded. So, it creates time utility by supplying the goods at right time to the ultimate consumers.

(4) *Insurance:* Insurance reduces risks. Business is subject to risks and uncertainties. These are inevitable in the field of business. Risks may be due to fire, theft, accident or any other natural calamity. Insurance companies who act as risk bearer cover risks. Insurance tries to reduce risks by spreading them out over a great number of people. The rate of premium depends upon the types of risks and the period for which the risk is covered.

(5) *Banking:* Banking solves the problem of finance. Businessmen receive money and also pay money in large amounts. It is risky to carry large amount of cash from one place to another. Here comes banking as a solution. Banking and financial institutions solve the problem of payment and facilitate exchange between buyer and seller.

The businessmen may also require short-term and long-term funds. Banks provide such finance to businessmen. Banks also advance loans in the form of overdraft, cash credit and discounting of bills of exchange.

(6) *Advertising:* Advertising fills the knowledge gap and it solves the difficulty of information. Exchange of goods and services is possible only if producers can bring the products to the consumers. Advertising and publicity are important media of mass communication. Advertising helps the consumers to know about the various products manufactured by manufacturers. The media used to advertise products are radio, newspapers, magazines, T.V. Internet and many more.

(7) *Salesmanship:* It facilitates personal selling. Many a times sales force is required to book orders directly from dealers or customers. Salesmanship is very much required in the sales of services and industrial goods. Again the sales force plays an important role in direct marketing, especially in the case of selling insurance policies.

(8) *Mercantile Agents:* Mercantile agents are middlemen who form a link between the buyers and sellers. They do not carry on business in their own name. In the process of distribution, producers and consumers are unable to have direct contact, as consumers are spread over a vast area. Mercantile agents remove this difficulty of personal contact. There are several types of mercantile agents such as brokers, commission agents, auctioneers, underwriters, insurers, etc.

(9) *Trade Promotion Organization in a Country:* They attend to difficulties of promotion and development of trade at national level. These are the organizations established by the business community to protect and promote their interest. They play promotional and developmental role for members. They do market research work, act as a clearing house of information, put their grievances before the government, make representation, and help business community in many ways. The examples include Chambers of Commerce, Export Promotion Councils, Indian Institute of Packaging, etc.

(10) *Global Organizations for International Trade:* They attend to promotion and development of trade at international level. The

main objective of global organizations is to promote international trade. The helps exporters and importers by collecting information about international marketing trends. The examples of such global organizations are World Bank, IMF, WTO, etc.

Advantages and Disadvantages of Aids-to-trade

Advantages

(1) Enable developing countries, particularly least developed countries (LDCs), to use trade more effectively to promote growth, development and poverty reduction and to achieve their developmental objectives, including the Millennium Development Goals (MDGs).
(2) Help developing countries, particularly least developed countries (LDCs), to build supply side capacity and trade related infrastructure in order to facilitate their access to markets and to export more.
(3) Help to facilitate, implement and adjust to trade reform and liberalization.
(4) Help to assist in regional, cultural integration.
(5) Promotes smooth integration between the different countries and to the world trading system.
(6) Promotes for growth and development of national as well as international trade agreements and their implementation.

Disadvantages

(1) Insufficient trade mainstreaming in national development strategies.
(2) Lack of private sector involvement in identifying trade needs.
(3) Limited absorptive capacity in recipient countries.
(4) Unpredictable donor response to trade priorities.
(5) Slow and bureaucratic processes and delivery mechanisms for rolling out trade-related assistance.
(6) Lack of data on trade policies and their development impact.
(7) Lack of easily available information on existing aids for trade instrument
(8) Ineffective monitoring and impact of assessment of trade related policies and activities.
(9) Limited support for regional, sub-regional and cross-border trade related programmes and policies.

(10) Inadequate support to address the adjustment cost of trade or liberalization.

POINTS TO REMEMBER

Meaning of business : It is an organized activity of an intuition of producing goods and services to earn profits.

Meaning of profession : It is an occupation which involves the rendering of services of specialized nature out of the expert knowledge of an individual.

Distinction between business and profession

	Business	Profession
1.	Establishment: It deals with goods and services	It deals with producing and distribution of services
2.	Operations: Production and distribution of goods and services	Rendering the personalized professional services To provide services
3.	Motive: To earn profit	
4.	Qualities: It is essential	It is very essential
5.	Investment: It is huge	Less capital is enough
6.	Reward: Profit	Salary/Remuneration
7.	Transferability of Interest: Ownership of goods is transferred	Not accessible ownership of knowledge

Classification

(a) Industries: Group of many business concerns
(b) Commerce: It is a bundle of activities which are essential to the industry

Trade

It is buying and selling of goods and services.

Aids to trade

(a) Transportation
(b) Warehouse
(c) Insurance
(d) Advertising
(e) Banking

Importance of business

Organized activity which aims at earning the profit through delighting the customer (explanation of this paragraph in required)

Objectives of business

(a) Economic : Related to finance
(b) Society: Related to society
(c) Human: Related to human beings
(d) Natural: Related to nature
(e) Global: Related to world as a whole

Vision

It is the goal of a businessman.

Mission

It is the organized activities to achieve the vision of a business organization.

Primary industry

It is the basic industry, related to natural resources.

Secondary industries

(a) Analytical
(b) Synthetic
(c) Processing
(d) Assembling
(e) Tertiary

Commence

Group of activities which helps in the process of trade.

Importance

It is essential to carry out all types of business activities [earlier points of activities must be expanded in detail].

Trade

It is the process of buying and selling of goods and services in exchange for money.

Aids to trade

These consist of:

(a) Transportation
(b) Communication
(c) Warehousing
(d) Insurance
(e) Banking
(f) Advertising
(g) Salesmanship
(h) Mercantile agent
(i) Trade business
(j) Global organization

Advantages of trade and aids to trade.
[Each point must be explained in detail].

QUESTION BANK

Section A (2 marks)

(1) Define the term business?
(2) What is meant by profession?
(3) What is meant by the term "industry"?
(4) Define trade?
(5) What are aids to trade?
(6) Define the term vision?
(7) Define the term mission?
(8) What is commerce?
(9) Give any two activities of trade?
(10) Give any two activities of aids-to-trade?

Section B

Analytical/Descriptive questions

(1) Distinguish between business and profession?
(2) Analyze the importance of business?
(3) Analyze the nature of business?

(4) Analyze the objectives of business?
(5) Bring out the comparison between business, profession and employment?
(6) Discuss the importance of commerce?
(7) What are aids-to-trade? How are these important to trade related activities? Discuss.

Section C

Essay type questions

(1) Explain the characteristic features of business?
(2) Explain the role of primary and secondary industries in building the nation?
(3) Analyze the role of transportation in trade?
(4) Explain the advantages and disadvantages of aids-to-trade?

Unit 2

Forms of Business Organization

Forms of business organisations – Nature and characteristics – significance – Sole proprietorship – Joint Hindu Family business – Partnership firm –Types – Co-operative society – Characteristics – Advantages and Disadvantages.

LEARNING OBJECTIVES

This chapter takes the reader to all types of business organizations, their merits and demerits, so that it helps the reader to evaluate his potential in stauting and understanding the type and business firms.

A Business Organization refers to any industrial, commercial or service organization which produces goods and/or services for sale or engages in distributing or assists in the process thereof. It is to represent any collection of business resources – factories, warehousing, machinery, material, employee, etc. and the planned use of which is limited within the framework of one man business, partnership, company, are other forms of business organization. In the words of Richard Norman Owens "A business organization is an enterprise engaged in the production or distribution of goods for sale in a market or rendering services for a price". In the words of Bayard O Wheeler " A business firm is an institution, company or enterprise engaged in buying and selling or being owned by one person or group of persons, who manage it within certain laid down creative policies".

2

Forms of Business Organization

Characteristics and Nature of Business Organization

(1) An association of persons or group
(2) A pluralistic institution
(3) Different forms
(4) Wide scope of activities
(5) Coordination of resources

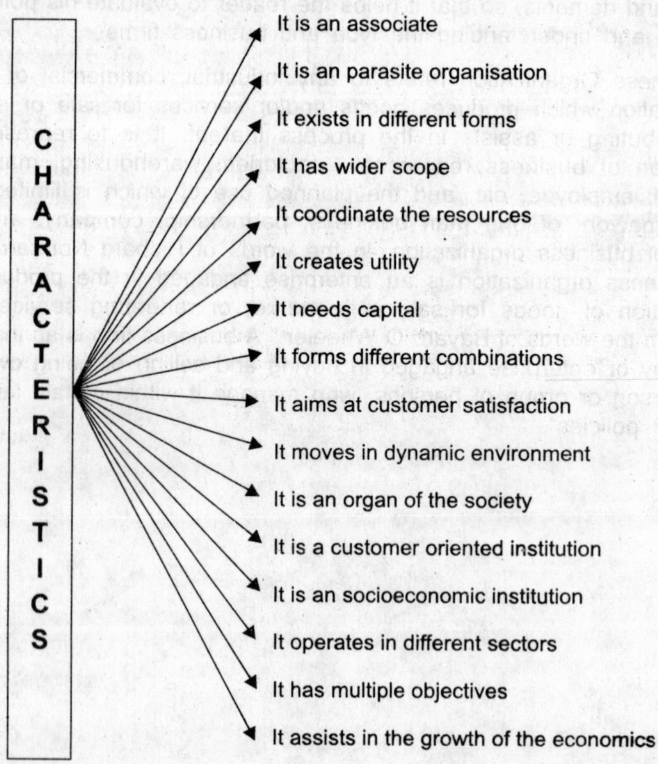

(6) Creates utilities
(7) Intensity of capital
(8) Increasing trends in forming into combination
(9) Customer satisfaction
(10) Dynamic environment
(11) It is a system an organ of the society
(12) Customer orientation
(13) Socioeconomic institution
(14) Operating in different sectors of the economy
(15) An institution with multiple objectives
(16) Faster growth of service organization
(17) Global operation
(18) Independent and separate role of entrepreneur and manager
(19) Innovation and marketing as basic function
(20) Government control and regulation
(21) Improves the standard of living of people

Significance of Business Organization

The significance of business may be classified into the following four categories, namely:

(1) Significance to National Economy
(2) Significance to Business Itself
(3) Significance to Community
(4) Significance from Other Points of View

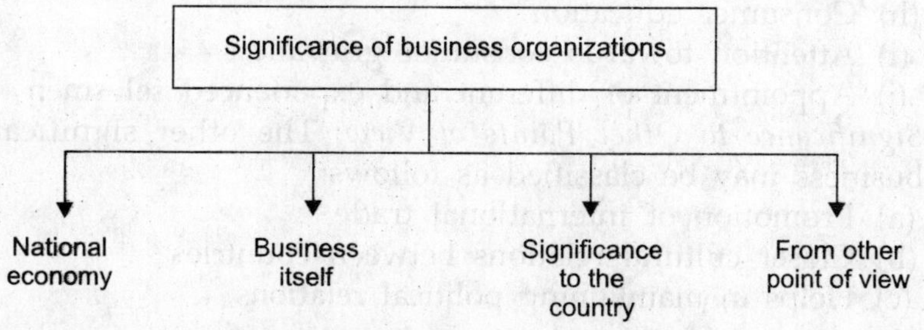

(1) *Significance to National Economy:* The significance of business to a nation may be expressed by the following facts:
  (a) Optimum and profitable use of resources
  (b) Balance industrial growth
  (c) Source of national income
  (d) Faster economic growth in the country
  (e) Contributes to national prosperity
  (f) Better utilization of human resources
  (g) Increase in the standard of living of the people

(h) Source for meeting import requirement
(i) To meet the obligations of development planning
(j) Large creation of employment
(k) Eradication of employment
(l) Capital formation
(m) Development of labour and capital market

(2) *Significance to Business Itself:* The significance of business from the point of view of business itself may be stated as below:
(a) Large-scale production and efficient distribution
(b) Creation of healthy competition
(c) Fulfilment of social responsibility
(d) Decrease in cost of production
(e) Helps to develop managerial staff
(f) Greater utilization of production capacities
(g) Development of the undertaking
(h) Profitable sales volume
(i) Specialization in production

(3) *Significance to Community:* The significance of business from the point of view of community may be stated as below:
(a) Uplifts the standard and quality of life
(b) Development of labour markets
(c) Human prosperity
(d) Creation of employment
(e) Creates habits of saving
(f) Provides goods and services at reasonable prices
(g) Advantages of form, place, time, and possession utilities
(h) Consumer education
(i) Attention towards consumer grievances
(j) Appointment of different and experienced salesmen

(4) *Significance to Other Points of View:* The other significance of business may be classified as follows:
(a) Promotion of international trade
(b) Closer cultural relations between countries
(c) Helps in maintaining political relations.

FORMS OF BUSINESS ORGANIZATIONS

Sole Proprietorship

A sole proprietorship is the oldest and the most common form of business. It is a one-man organization where a single individual owns, manages and controls the business. In other words, when ownership and management of business are in control of one individual, it is known as 'Sole Proprietorship' or 'Sole Tradership'. It is seen everywhere

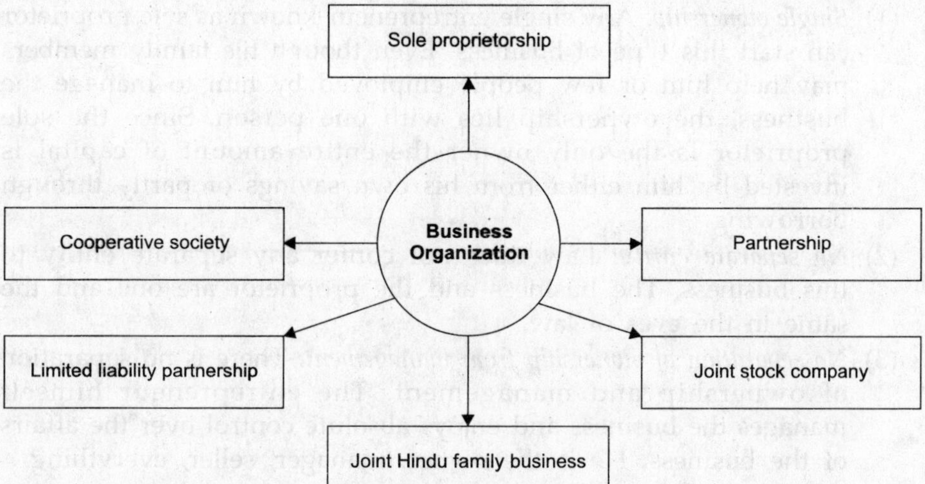

in every country, every state, every locality. The shops or stores which you see in your locality the grocery shop, the vegetable shop, the sweets shop the chemist shop, the paanwala, the stationery shop, STD/ ISD telephone booths, etc. come under sole proprietorship. It is not that a sole tradership business must be a small one. The volume of activities of such a business unit may be quite large. However, since it is owned and managed by one single individual, often the size of business remains small.

Characteristics of Sole Traders or Sole Proprietorship

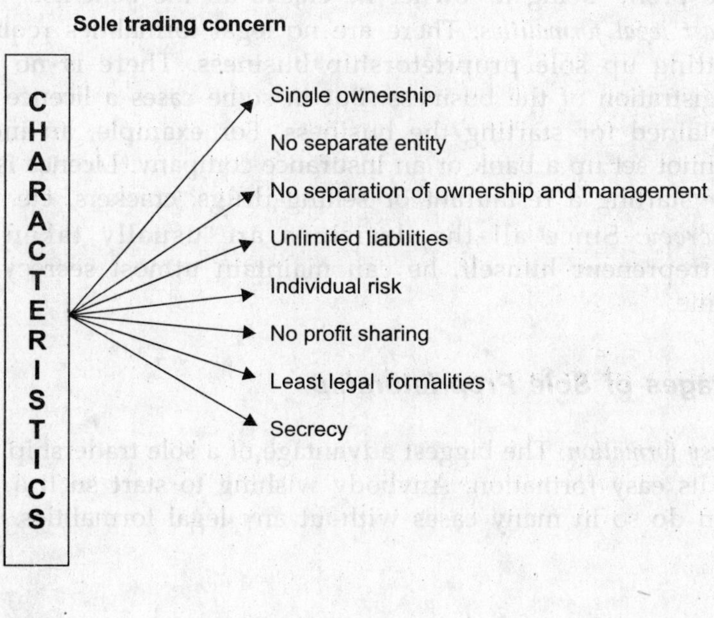

(1) *Single ownership:* Any single entrepreneur known as sole proprietor can start this type of business. Even though his family members may help him or few people employed by him to manage the business, the ownership lies with one person. Since the sole proprietor is the only owner the entire amount of capital is invested by him either from his own savings or partly through borrowing.

(2) *No separate entity:* Law does not confer any separate entity to this business. The business and the proprietor are one and the same in the eyes of law.

(3) *No separation of ownership from management:* There is no separation of ownership and management. The entrepreneur himself manages the business and enjoys absolute control over the affairs of the business. He is the owner, manager, seller, everything.

(4) *Unlimited liability:* The liability of the sole proprietor is unlimited. Thus, the private property of the owner is at risk as it is liable for business obligation in the event of business losses. There will be hardly any difference between personal property and business property of the entrepreneur.

(5) *Individual risk:* The entire risk of the business is borne by the entrepreneur himself as he is the only owner of the business. All the risks and gains are the sole responsibility of the owner. This undivided risk will keep the entrepreneur vigilant and cautious for the business.

(6) *No profit sharing:* The entrepreneur enjoys the entire profit earned in this form of business as there are no other persons to share the profit. Being its owner he enjoys all the benefits.

(7) *Least legal formalities:* There are no legal formalities required for setting up sole proprietorship business. There is no need of registration of the business. But in some cases a licence is to be obtained for starting the business. For example, an individual cannot set up a bank or an insurance company. Licence is needed for starting a restaurant or selling drugs, crackers, etc.

(8) *Secrecy:* Since all the decisions are usually taken by the entrepreneur himself, he can maintain utmost secrecy for the same.

Advantages of Sole Proprietorship

(1) *Easy formation:* The biggest advantage of a sole tradership business is its easy formation. Anybody wishing to start such a business can do so in many cases without any legal formalities.

(2) *Better control:* The owner has full control over his business. He plans, organizes, coordinates its various activities. Since, he has all authority, there is always effective control.

(3) *Prompt decision-making:* As the sole owner takes all the decisions himself, the decision-making is quick, which enables the owner to take care of available opportunities immediately and provide immediate solutions to problems.

(4) *Flexibility in operation:* One man ownership and control makes it possible for change in operations to be brought about or/and when necessary.

(5) *Retention of business secrets:* Another important advantage of a sole proprietorship business is that the owner is in a position to maintain absolute secrecy regarding his business activities.

(6) *Direct motivation:* The owner is directly motivated to put his best efforts as he alone is the beneficiary of the profits earned.

(7) *Personal attention to customer needs:* In a sole tradership business one generally finds the proprietor taking personal care of consumer needs as he normally functions within a small geographical area.

(8) *Creation of employment:* A sole tradership business facilitates self-employment and also employment for many others. It promotes entrepreneurial skills among the individuals.

(9) *Social benefits:* A sole proprietor is the master of his own business. He has absolute freedom in taking decisions using his skill and capability. This gives him high self-esteem and dignity in the society and gradually he acquires several social virtues like self-reliance, self-determination, independent thought and action, initiative, hard work, etc. Thus, he sets an example for others to follow.

(10) *Equitable distribution of wealth:* A sole proprietorship business is generally a small-scale business. Hence, there is opportunity for many individuals to own and manage small business units. This enables widespread dispersion of economic wealth and diffuses concentration of business in the hands of a few.

Disadvantages of Sole Proprietorship

(1) *Unlimited liability:* In sole proprietorship the liability of business is recovered from the personal assets of the owner. It restricts the sole trader to take more risk and increase the volume of his business.

(2) *Limited financial resources:* The ability to raise and borrow money by one individual is always limited. The inadequacy of finance is a major handicap for the growth of sole proprietorship firm.

(3) *Limited capacity of individual:* An individual has limited knowledge and skills. Thus, his capacity to undertake responsibilities, his capacity to manage to take decisions and to bear the risks of business are also limited.

(4) *Uncertainty of duration:* The existence of a sole proprietorship business is linked with the life of the proprietor. Illness, death, or insolvency of the owner brings an end to the business. The continuity of business operation is, therefore, uncertain.

JOINT HINDU FAMILY BUSINESS (JHF)

The JHF business is a form of business organization found only in India. In this form of business, all the members of a Hindu undivided family own the business jointly. The affairs of business are managed by the head, who is known as 'KARTA'.

A JHF business comes into existence as per the Hindu inheritance laws of India. In a Joint Hindu Family business only the male members get a share in the business by virtue of them being part of the family. The membership is limited up to three successive generations. Thus, an individual, his son(s) and his grandson(s) become the members of a Joint Hindu Family by birth. They are also called 'coparceners'. The term coparceners implies that such an individual has got the right to ask for a partition of the JHF business and to have his separate share. A daughter has no right to ask for a partition and is, therefore, not a coparcener.

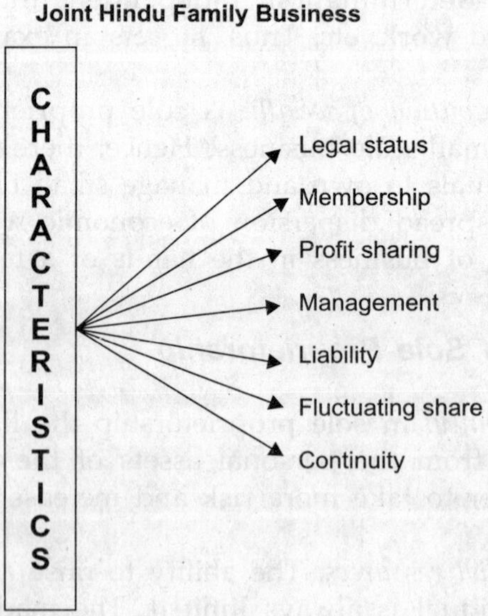

Characteristics of JHF Business

(1) *Legal status:* The Joint Hindu Family business is a jointly owned business just like a jointly owned property. It is governed by Hindu Law. It can enter into partnership agreement with others.

(2) *Membership:* There is no membership other than the members of the joint family. Inside the family also, it is restricted only to male members who are coparceners by birth.

(3) *Profit sharing:* All coparceners have equal share in the profits of the business. In the event of death of any of the coparceners, his wife can claim share of profit.

(4) *Management:* The management of a JHF is in the hands of the senior-most family member who is known as the 'KARTA'. He has the authority to manage the business and his ways of managing cannot be questioned by the coparceners.

(5) *Liability:* The liability of each member of the JHF business is limited to the extent of his share in the business. But the liability of the KARTA is unlimited as it extends to his personal property.

(6) *Fluctuating share:* The individual share of each coparcener keeps on fluctuating. This is because every birth of a male child in the family adds to the number of coparceners and every death of a coparcener reduces the number.

(7) *Continuity:* A JHF business continues to exist on the death of any coparcener. Even on the death of the KARTA, it continues to exist as the next seniormost family member become the KARTA. However, a JHF business can be dissolved any time either through mutual agreement between members or by partition.

Advantages of JHF Business

(1) *Assured share in profits:* Every coparcener is assured a share in the profits irrespective of his contribution to the successful running of the business. This, in a way, safeguards the interests of some members of the family like minors, sick, disabled and widows.

(2) *Freedom in Managing:* The KARTA enjoys full freedom in conducting the family business. It enables him to take quick decisions without much interference.

(3) *Sharing of knowledge and experience:* A JHF business provides opportunity for the young members of the family to get the benefit of knowledge and experience of the elder members and also helps in inculcating virtues like discipline, self-sacrifice, tolerance, etc.

(4) *Unlimited liability of the KARTA:* The liability of the coparceners is limited, except for that of the KARTA. This makes the KARTA to manage the business in the most efficient manner.

(5) *Continued existence:* A JHF business is not affected by the insolvency or death of any member including that KARTA. Thus, it can continue for a long period of time.

Disadvantages of JHF Business

(1) *Limited resources:* JHF business has generally limited financial and managerial resources. Therefore, it cannot undertake big and risky business.
(2) *Lack of motivation:* There is always lack of motivation among the members to work hard. It is because the benefit of hard work does not go entirely to any individual member but shared by all the coparceners.
(3) *Scope for misuse of power by the KARTA:* Since the KARTA has absolute freedom to manage the business, there is scope for him to misuse it for his personal gains. An inefficient KARTA can also harm the business.
(4) *Scope for conflict:* In a Joint Hindu Family business, the male members of three successive generations are involved. It may leads to conflict between coparceners.
(5) *Instability:* The continuity of business is always under threat. It may be due to a small rift within the family and if a coparcener asks far partition, the business is closed.

PARTNERSHIP FIRM

A partnership firm is a form of organization where two or more persons associate to run a business with a view to earn profit. Persons from similar background or persons of different ability and skills, may join together to carry on a business. Each member of such a group is individually known as 'Partner' and collectively the firms are known as a 'Partnership firms'. These firms are governed by the Indian Partnership Act, 1932.

Characteristics

(1) *Number of partners:* There should be more than one person to form a partnership. But there is restriction for the maximum number of partners. In case of ordinary business, the partners must not exceed 20 and in case of banking must not exceed 10 (before nationalization).
(2) *Agreement:* There must be an agreement between the parties concerned. This is the most important characteristic of partnership

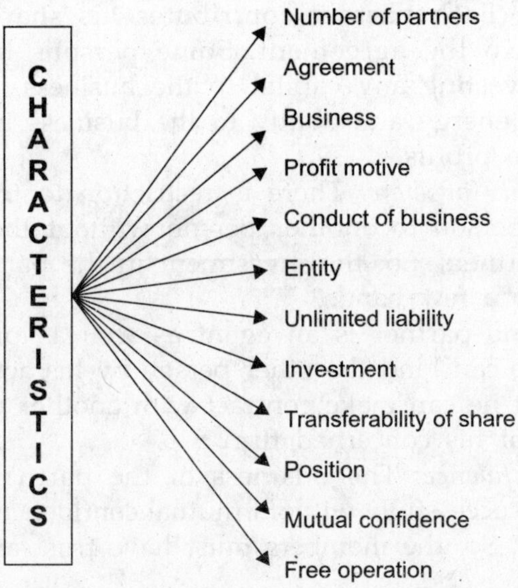

firms. Without agreement, partnership cannot be formed. "No agreement no partnership". But only competent persons are entitled to make a contract. There are some provisions contained in the partnership agreement. These are determined clearly before the commencement of business. But it differs from business to business. This document must be written so that disputes may be settled according the provisions of the contract or agreement.

(3) *Business:* The object of the formation of partnership is to carry on any type of business. It may be manufacturing, or merchandise type small or large-scale business. But it should not be illegal.

(4) *Profit motive:* The basic motive of the formation of partnership is to earn profit. Thus, profit is distributed among the partners according to agreed proportion. If there is loss, it will be sustained by all partners except minor.

(5) *Conduct of business:* The business of partnership is conducted by all the partners or any of them acting for all. But each partner is allowed to participate in the management by law.

(6) *Entity:* It has no separate entity apart from its members. It is not independent of the partners. Law has not granted it any legal entity.

(7) *Unlimited liability:* This is a prominent feature of partnership that the liability of each partner is not limited to the amount invested but his private property is also liable to pay the business obligations.

(8) *Investment:* Each partner contributes his share in the capital according to the agreement. Some persons become partners without investing any capital to the business. But they devote their time, energy and ability to the business instead of capital and receive profits.

(9) *Transferability of share:* There is restriction to transfer the share from one person to another person without the consent of the existing partners. So, the investment in the partnership remains confined to a few hands.

(10) *Position:* One partner is an agent as well as principal to other partner. He can bind the other person by his act. In the position of an agent he can make contract with another person or parties on behalf of his concerned firm.

(11) *Mutual confidence:* The business of the partnership cannot be conducted successfully without mutual confidence and cooperation of partners. So, the members must have trust and confidence in each other.

(12) *Free operation:* There are no strict rules and regulations to control the partnership activities in our country, i.e., no restriction for the audit of accounts, submission of various reports and other copies to any government authority. So, this organization may operate freely without any interference.

Advantages of Partnership Firm

(1) *Easy formation:* A partnership can be formed without many legal formalities and expenses. Every partnership firm need not be registered.

(2) *Larger resources:* As compared to sole proprietorship, a partnership business firm can pool large financial resources. Thus, it can enter into bigger operations and can have more credit facilities. It can also have better managerial talent.

(3) *Flexibility in operation:* There is flexibility of operation in partnership business due to limited number of partners. These partners can change their operations and amend objectives if necessary by mutual consent.

(4) *Better management:* Partners take more interest in the affairs of business as there is a direct relationship, between ownership, control and profit. They can discuss the affairs of business and can take prompt decision.

(5) *Sharing of risk:* In partnership, risk of loss is easier to bear by individual partners as it is shared by all the partners.

(6) *Production of minority interest:* Every partner has an equal say in decision-making. A partner can present a decision being taken if it adversely affects his interests. In extreme cases, a dissenting partner may withdraw from partnership and can dissolve it.

(7) *Better public relation:* In a partnership firm, the group managing the affairs of the firm is generally small. It facilitates cordial relationship with the public.

Disadvantages of Partnership Firm

(1) *Instability:* A partnership firm does not continue to exist indefinitely. The death, insolvency or lunacy of a partner may bring about an unexpected end to partnership.

(2) *Unlimited liability:* As the liability of partners is joint and several to an unlimited extent, any one of the partners can be called upon to pay all the debts even from his personal properties. Further, as every partner has a right to take part in the management of the firm, any wrong decision by a single partner may lead to heavy liabilities for others.

(3) *Lack of harmony:* Since every partner has equal right, there are greater possibilities of friction and quarrel among the partners. Differences of opinion may lead to mistrust and disharmony which may ultimately result in disruption and closure of the firm.

(4) *Limited capital:* As there is a restriction on the maximum number of partners, the capital which can be raised is limited.

Types of Partnership

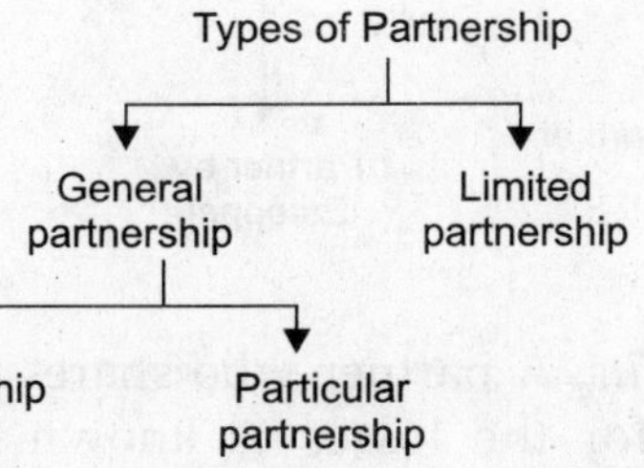

(1) *General partnership:* In this type of partnership, partners are with unlimited liabilities. It can be further divided into two types:
   (a) *Partnership at will:* Mutual trust, faith and confidence among partners are the keys for the existence of this type of partnership.
   (b) *Particular partnership:* It is formed for a fixed duration or for specific tasks and it dissolves automatically as soon the fixed time lapses or the specific task is achieved.

(2) *Limited partnership:* All the partners in this type of partnership have limited liability except one partner.

(3) *Active partner:* Partner who takes an active role in the management of the business is called active partner. He is also called 'actual' or 'ostensible' partner. He is an agent of the other partners in the ordinary course of business of the firm and considered a full-fledged partner in the real sense of the term.

(4) *Sleeping or dormant partner:* A sleeping or dormant partner is one who does not take any active part in the management of the business. He contributes capital and shares the profits which is usually less than that of the active partners. He is liable for all. The relationship with the firm is not disclosed to the general public.

(5) *Nominal partner:* A partner who simply lends his name to the firm is called nominal partner. He neither contributes any capital nor shares in the profits nor take part in the management of the business. But he is liable to third parties like other partners. A nominal partner must be distinguished from the sleeping partner. While the nominal partner is known to the outsiders and does not share in the profits, the sleeping partner shares in the profit and his relationship is kept secret.

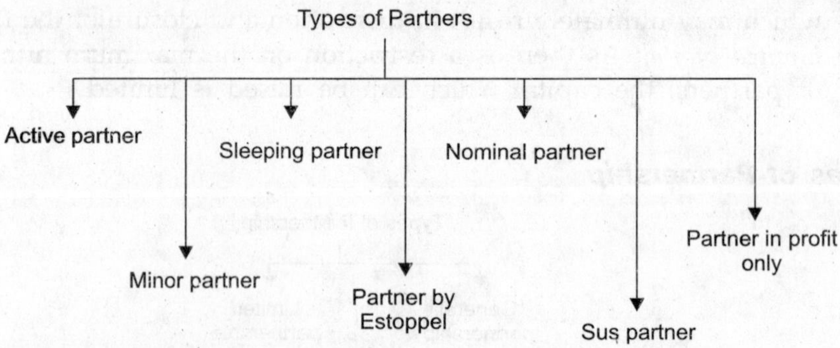

(6) *Partner in profits:* A partner who shares in the profits only without being liable for the losses is known as partner in profits. He does not take part in the management of the business but he is liable to third parties for all the debts of the firm.

(7) *Sub-partner:* When a stranger shares the profits derived from the firm by a partner, he is regarded as a sub-partner. A sub-partner is in no way connected with the firm or he is not a partner of the firm. He is simply a partner's partner. Therefore, he has no rights against the firm nor he is liable for the debts of the firm. He only shares profits from a partner.

(8) *Partner by estoppel or holding out:* When a partner is not a partner but represents to the outside world that he is a partner in a firm, he is stopped or prevented from denying the truth. He is considered a partner in the eyes of law. Similarly, if a person is declared to be a partner by a partner of a firm and such person remained silent without denying it, he is also considered a partner by holding out. Thus, such persons are liable to outsiders and the partners on the principle of estoppel or holding out because on faith of their representation action to outsiders have granted credit to the firm.

(9) *Minor partner:* Partnership arises from contract and a minor is not competent to enter into contract. Therefore, strictly speaking, a minor cannot be a full-fledged partner. But with the consent of all the partners, he can be admitted into partnership for benefits only. He is not personally liable to third parties for the debts of the firm. On attaining majority, if he continues as a partner, his liability will become unlimited with effect from the date of original admission into the firm.

COOPERATIVE SOCIETY

The forms of business ownership and organization discussed so far are run basically with a view to make profit. The cooperative form of organization is different from the rest in so far as it is not set up with profit as the guiding motive but with the main purpose of rendering service to its members in particular and to the society in general. Cooperative organizations have emerged primarily to protect and safeguard the economic interest of the relatively weaker sections of the society in the face of exploitation by businessman whose primary motive is profit maximization.

Meaning

According to the International Labour Office, a cooperative organization is:

> "an association of persons, usually of limited means, who have voluntarily joined together to achieve a common economic end, through the formation of a democratically controlled business organization, making equitable contributions to the capital required and accepting a fair share of risks and benefits of the undertaking".

Characteristics of Cooperative Organization

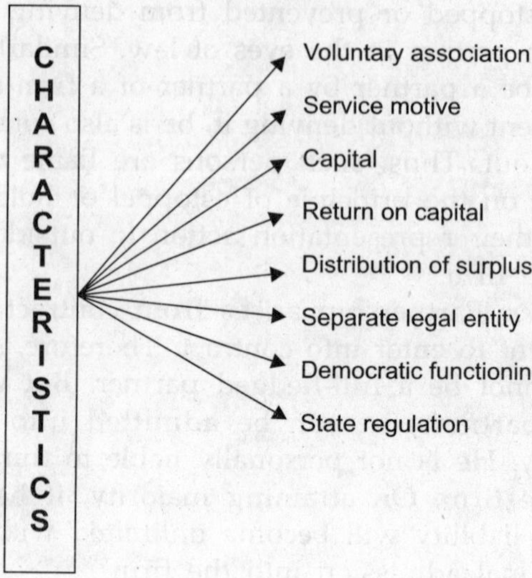

The cooperative organization being different in its rationale and philosophy possesses certain features and characteristics which may be briefly explained as follows:

(1) *Voluntary association:* As stated above, persons desirous of pursuing a common objective can form themselves into an association and leave the same as and when one likes by withdrawing his capital. Thus, voluntary feature of the cooperative organization has two important connotations:

(i) Any person may become a member of such an organization irrespective of his caste, creed, religion, colour, sex, etc., and

(ii) The members come together to form themselves into an association without any coercion or intimidation.

(2) *Service motive:* As stated earlier, a cooperative organization is established primarily with a view to rendering service to its members in particular and to the society in general. This, however, does not mean that such an organization will not work for profit. There are several cooperative organizations which are making reasonably good profits. It gives more emphasis on service and not on profits.

(3) *Capital:* The capital of the cooperative organization is procured from its members in the form of share capital. However, the share capital constitutes only a limited source of business finance, the major part of which is raised by the cooperative organization

either by way of loan from the government and the apex cooperative institution or by way of grants and assistance from the government.

(4) *Return on capital:* The return on capital subscribed by the members is in the form of a fixed rate of dividend which is a charge on the trading surplus of the organization.

(5) *Distribution of surplus:* The entire trading surplus earned by a cooperative organization after meeting its trading expenses and paying a fixed rate of dividend is not distributed among the members. Under the present law governing cooperative organizations, a sum total ¼ of its profits to be transferred to general reserves. Similarly, a portion of the profits not exceeding 10% may be utilized for the general welfare of the society's functioning. The rest of the surplus may be distributed in the form of bonus on a certain agreed basis but not on the basis of the capital contributed by the members. The bonus may be paid to the members in proportion to the purchase made during the year by the members in case of consumers' cooperative stores, or in proportion to the goods delivered for sale to the society in the case of producer's cooperative store.

(6) *Separate legal entity:* Like a company, a cooperative organization also enjoys a separate and independent entity distinct from that of its members. As such, it has a perpetual life and is not affected by the entry and exit of members. It can sue in its own name. It can own property and dispose it of in its own name, likewise can enter into business contracts in its own name.

(7) *Democratic functioning:* The management of cooperative organization vests in a managing committee elected by members on the basis of "one-member-one-vote" irrespective of the number of shares held by any member. It is the general body of the members which lays down the broad framework of policy within which the managing committee has to function.

(8) *State regulation:* A cooperative organization right from its inception up to its end is subjected to detailed regulation under the Co-operative Societies, Act 1919 or other State Co-operative Societies Act. A cooperative organization in order to be registered with Registrar of Co-operative Societies has to fulfil certain requirements.

Types of Cooperative Societies

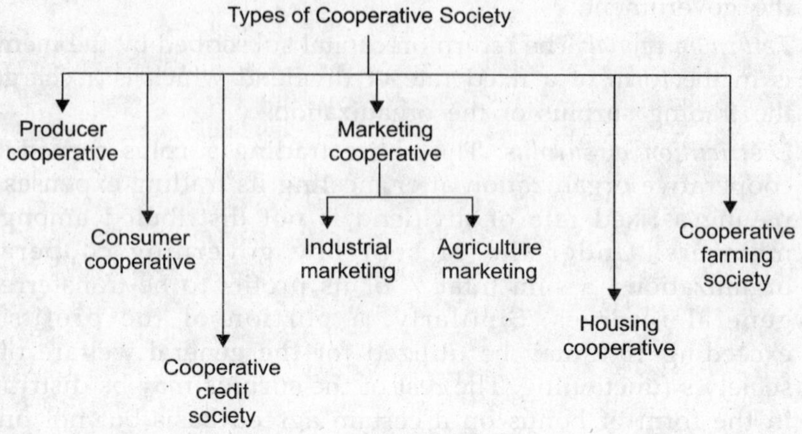

On the basis of nature of services rendered by cooperatives, they may be classified into the following categories:

(1) *Producer cooperatives:* These cooperative societies are formed to help and strengthen small producers who cannot face the competition offered by organized large-scale producers. These cooperatives may be organized in one of the following two basis:

(a) The producer members maintain their separate individual entity. The society supplies them with raw materials, tools, equipment, etc. The members sell their individual output to the society.

(b) The member producers produce on behalf of the society as its employees. The member producers are paid wages for their work. Here, again the society supplies them with raw materials, tools and equipment, etc. In either case, the marketing of the products is undertaken by the society.

(2) *Consumer cooperatives:* These cooperatives are formed for the main purpose of making available day-to-day requirements for goods to their members at cheaper prices. For this purpose, they buy their goods from wholesaler at wholesale prices and sell them to members and often to non-members as well at price lower than the market prices. The difference between the wholesale price and the selling price of the cooperatives represents the surplus which after meeting the expenses are distributed among the members as bonus, besides transferring a part thereof to general reserve and other kinds of reserves. This form of cooperative has been receiving government's attention and help with a view to contributing the general problem of price rise.

(3) *Marketing cooperatives:* These societies are set up either for selling manufactured products or products of agricultural commodities. As such, marketing cooperatives may be classified into two broad categories:

(a) *Industrial marketing cooperatives:* These societies pool the manufactured products of small producers such as artisans, weavers, small producers, etc. and sell them at prices which are remunerative to the member producers.

(b) *Agricultural marketing cooperative:* These are organized by farmers for selling their own farm product and also for obtaining their agricultural inputs. Thus, agricultural cooperatives are engaged in two-way function of selling farm products and buying seeds, manures, implements and many other goods. Since agricultural marketing involves several steps like processing, warehousing, financing, etc., these cooperatives are often formed on a multipurpose basis for catering to the needs of agriculturists both as sellers and buyers of products.

(4) *Cooperative credit societies:* These are formed by members to pool their savings and to invest their resources thus collected for giving loans to members on favourable terms involving interests, security and repayment. Such cooperatives are organized both in rural and urban areas. In rural areas, these are called primary credit societies or rural credit societies while in urban areas these are known as cooperative banks.

(5) *Housing cooperatives:* These societies are formed by those people who strive to own a flat or a piece of land for constructing their own house. As such, these activities are formed mostly in urban areas and that too in big cities where the problem of hosting is acute. These societies are allotted land (developed or underdeveloped) by local authority or by the Urban Development Authority at concessional prices. The same is true with regard to the allotment of flats. Such societies can also negotiate loans for its members on easy terms from financial institutions and national building organization which have been recently established. They may also procure building materials in bulk for their members so as to reap the economies of bulk buying.

(6) *Cooperative farming societies:* In our country, the problem of subdivision and fragmentation of agricultural landholdings is very acute. One of the ways to get over this problem is to organize small landowners and tillers of land into farming societies with a view to reaping the benefits of large-scale mechanical farming. This large-scale cooperative farming results into raising agricultural output and reducing the cost per unit.

Advantages of Cooperative Societies

Different types of cooperatives have distinct merits to their credit. But there are some common merits which can be witnessed in all cooperatives. These are as follows:

(1) *Easy formation:* Being a voluntary association, it is easy to form as it does not require long and complicated legal preliminaries. Any 10 adult persons can voluntarily form themselves into an association and get it registered with the Registrar of Cooperatives.

(2) *Democratic functioning:* As observed earlier, the management of cooperatives is vested in a managing committee which is elected by the general members of the cooperative on the basis of 'one-man-one-vote'. As such, it does not matter whether a member holds one share or more than one share.

(3) *Limited liability:* Like the liability of the shareholders in company form of organization, the liability of the members in a cooperative organization is also limited to their capital contribution. The effect of limited liability is mentioned in the bye-laws of the co-operative which is checked by the Registrar at the time of registering the same.

(4) *Internal vitality:* Cooperatives are not permitted to declare dividend for its members exceeding certain limits, the balance of the surplus earned in any year by the co-operative can well be utilized for its growth, modernization and development. Thus there is build-in advantage of ploughing back of profits for the profits for the better health and prosperity of the organization.

(5) *Continuity:* Like the company, the cooperative enjoys a separate legal entity of its own independent of the entity of its members who own it. Hence, the life of cooperative organization remains unaffected by the death, insolvency, or conviction of a member.

(6) *State assistance:* Since cooperatives have been adopted by the government as an instrument of economic policy, grants, loans and financial assistance are offered to them to make them function efficiently.

(7) *Social service:* Cooperatives foster fellow feeling among members and impart moral and educational values in their everyday life which are essential for better living.

(8) *Reducing inequalities:* Since the benefits and profits of cooperatives are enjoyed by the people with moderate means, this helps in raising the economic status of the relatively poor people thereby reducing the disparity between the rich and the poor.

Disadvantages of Cooperative Societies

(1) *Limited capital:* The amount of capital that a cooperative can muster is limited because of the membership remaining confined to particular locality or region and also because of the principle of 'one-man-one-vote' and the dividend restrictions.

(2) *Plenty of state regulation:* Under the existing arrangements, the cooperatives are subjected to a variety of regulations from the cooperative department of the State Government partly because the state offers a number of financial helps and partly because it is always anxious to see that the movement succeeds. All this led to excessive state regulations in the day-to-day functioning of the cooperatives which, at times, amounts to interference.

(3) *Lack of managerial talent:* Cooperatives at the primary level generally suffer from extremely limited managerial talent because they depend on the personnel drawn from amongst their own members to serve on the managing committee which, in turn, manages the day-to-day affairs of the cooperatives. However, at the higher levels, namely, state and apex federation level, this constraint is not so acute. But if we compare the availability of managerial talent in a company form of organization, then again cooperatives do not stand anywhere near them.

(4) *Lack of secrecy:* As usually is common with the forms of organization which enjoy separate legal entity and as such are under obligation to make fuller disclosures of their operations to their members, the cooperatives too being corporate in status fail to preserve their business secrets. In this respect, cooperatives are similar to the company form of organization.

(5) *Lack of motivation:* The built-in constraint that cooperative societies cannot offer dividend beyond fixed rate (i.e., 6 ¼ per cent), the members of the managing committee with whom rests the responsibility of managing the cooperatives do not feel motivated to do their best to see the cooperative a grand success.

(6) *Differences among members:* Although cooperatives are formed with great fanfare and with great ideals of cooperation and self-help, but soon its higher values of human life disappear with the passage of time. These are often bickerings, differences and bad blood created among members on petty matters. This marks the beginning of an end to the cooperative organization.

LIMITED LIABILITY PARTNERSHIP

Limited Liability Partnership entities, the worldwide recognized form of business organization has been introduced in India by way of

Limited Liability Partnership Act, 2008. A Limited Liability Partnership, popularly known as LLP combines the advantages of both the Company and Partnership into a single form of organization.

In an LLP one partner is not responsible or liable for another partner's misconduct or negligence; this is an important difference from that of an unlimited partnership. In an LLP, all partners have a form of limited liability for each individual's protection within the partnership, similar to that of the shareholders of a corporation. However, unlike corporate shareholders, the partners have the right to manage the business directly. An LLP also limits the personal liability of a partner for the errors, omissions, incompetence, or negligence of the LLP's employees or other agents. Limited Liability Partnership is managed as per the LLP Agreement, however in the absence of such agreement the LLP would be governed by the framework provided in Schedule 1 of Limited Liability Partnership Act, 2008 which describes the matters relating to mutual rights and duties of partners of the LLP and of the limited liability partnership and its partners. LLP has a separate legal entity, liable to the full extent of its assets, the liability of the partners would be limited to their agreed contribution in the LLP. Further, no partner would be liable on account of the independent or unauthorized actions of other partners, thus allowing individual partners to be shielded from joint liability created by another partner's wrongful business decisions or misconduct.

Limited Liability Partnership Act, 2008 came into effect by way of notification dated 31st March 2009.

Advantages of Limited Liability Partnership

1. Renowned and accepted form of business worldwide in comparison to company.
2. Low cost of formation.
3. Easy to establish.
4. Easy to manage and run.
5. No requirement of any minimum capital contribution.
6. No restrictions as to maximum number of partners.
7. LLP and its partners are distinct from each other.
8. Partners are not liable for any act of partners.
9. Less compliance level.
10. No exposure to personal assets of the partners except in case of fraud.
11. Less requirement as to maintenance of statutory records.
12. Less government intervention.

13. Easy to dissolve or wind-up.
14. Professionals can form multi-disciplinary Professional LLP, which was not allowed earlier.

Disadvantages of Limited Liability Partnership

1. Audit requirement only in case of contributions exceeding Rs. 25 lakh or turnover exceeding Rs. 40 lakh.
2. Any act of the partner without the other partner, may bind the LLP.
3. Under some cases, liability may extend to personal assets of partners.
4. Cannot raise money from public.

POINTS TO REMEMBER

Business Objectives	:	It refers to any industrial, commercial or science organisation which produces goods and services for sale or engages in distributing process with a view to earn profits.
Characteristics	:	Explanation for each characteristic features is for section 'C' questions.
Significance	:	Natural economy-business itself to the connectivity from other point of view.
Sole Propertiorship	:	It is one man organization to earn profit by engaging in dealing with goods or services.
Characteristics	:	Explanation for each characteristic features is needed for section 'C' questions.
Joint Hindu Family Business	:	It is found only in India. In this form, all the members of a Hindu Undivided Family own the business jointly.
Characteristics	:	Explanations for each character is needed for section 'C' questions.
Partnership firm	:	It is a firm where two or more persons are associated to run a business with a new to earn profits.
Characteristics	:	Explanation for each characteristic features is needed for section 'C' questions.

Types of partnership

(a) General partnership: All the partners in this form of business firm have unlimited liability.
(b) Limited partnership: Except one, all other partners in this form of business firm have limited liability.

Types of partners

(a) Active partners
(b) Sleeping partners
(c) Nominal partner
(d) Partner in profits
(e) Secret partner
(f) Partner by estoppel
(g) Minor partner

Cooperative society	:	The main purpose of this organization is to render service and it is an association of voluntary members to protect their interest.
Characteristics	:	Explanation for each characteristic features in needed to answer section 'C' types of question.
Types of Cooperative Society	:	(1) Producers' cooperative (2) Consumer cooperative (3) Marketing cooperative (4) Cooperative credit societies (5) Housing cooperatives

Advantages and disadvantages of each from of business organization is needed to answer section 'B' or 'C' questions.

QUESTION BANK

Section A (2 marks)

Objective Type

(1) Define the term "Business Organization"?
(2) Give any two characteristic features of business organization?
(3) What is meant by sole trading concern?
(4) What is joint Hindu family business?

(5) What is meant by partnership firm?
(6) Who is a general partner?
(7) Who is a limited partner?
(8) Who is a active partner?
(9) Who is a sleeping partner?
(10) Who is a partner by Estoppel?
(11) Who is a nominal partner?
(12) Who is a minor partner?
(13) Give the meaning of the term "Cooperative Society".
(14) What is are producers cooperatives?
(15) What is meant by consumer cooperatives?
(16) What is meant marketing cooperatives?
(17) What is meant agricultural marketing cooperative?
(18) What is meant credit cooperative societies?
(19) What is meant housing cooperative societies?

Section B

Analytical or descriptive type questions

(1) Analyze the characteristic features of business organization.
(2) Analyze the characteristic features of sole trading concern.
(3) Analyze the existence of JHF business.
(4) Discuss the characteristics feature of a partnership firm.
(5) Analyze the characteristics feature of a cooperative society.
(6) Analyze the functioning of a cooperative societies today.
(7) "Cooperative societies are more relevant even in global environment". Discuss.
(8) "Joint Hindu Family Business" firms are vanishing today. Discuss.

Section C

Essay type questions

(1) Explain the characteristic features of business organization.
(2) Explain the characteristic features of sole trading concern.
(3) Explain the advantages and disadvantages of sole trading concern.
(4) Explain the features of Joint Hindu Family Business.
(5) Explain the features of partnership firms.
(6) Explain the advantages and disadvantages of partnership firm.

Unit 3
Joint Stock Company

Meaning – Characteristic Features – Types of Companies – Company Limited by Guarantee Holding Company – Formation of a Joint Stock Company – Types of Promoters

LEARNING OBJECTIVES

This chapter takes the reader to understand the basic concepts of Joint Stock Company. It enable the reader to establish joint stock company. It highlights the functioning of different types of promoters.

MEANING

In a partnership firm, we know that the number of partners cannot exceed 20. So, there is a limit to the contribution of capital. Secondly, even if the partners could contribute a large amount of capital, they would hesitate to do so considering the risk involved in business and their unlimited liability. A Joint Stock Company takes care of these two problems, organization is known. It is a voluntary association of persons who generally contribute capital to carry on a particular type of business, which is established by law and can be dissolved only by law. Persons who contribute capital become members of the company. This form of business has a legal existence separate from its members, which means even if its members die, the company remains in existence. This form of business organization generally requires huge capital investments, which is contributed by its members. The total capital of a joint stock company is called share capital and it is divided into a number of units called shares. Thus, every member has some shares in the business depending upon the amount of capital contributed by him. These members are also called shareholders.

3

Joint Stock Company

The companies in India are governed by the Indian Companies Act, 1956. The Act defines a company as an artificial person created by law, having a separate legal entity, with perpetual succession and a common seal.

DEFINITIONS OF JOINT STOCK COMPANY

Before starting a business in company form, the entrepreneur must possess detailed knowledge about the company. A good number of authors have defined the company in their own ways. Few important definitions are given below

(1) Prof. L.H. Haney: "A Joint Stock Company is a voluntary association of individuals for profit, having a capital divided into transferable shares, the ownership of which is the condition of membership."

(2) James Stephens: "A company is an association of many persons who contribute money or money's worth to a common stock and employ it in some trade or business, and who share the profit and loss arising therefrom."

(3) Chief Justice Marshall: "A corporation is an artificial being, invisible, intangible and existing only in the eyes of the law. Being a mere creature of law, it possesses only those properties which the charter of its creation confers upon it, either expressly or as incidental to its very existence."

(4) Indian Companies Act, 1956: According to Section 3 of Indian Companies Act-1956, "A company means a company formed and registered under this Act or an existing company." According to Clause (ii) of Section 3, "Existing company means a company formed and registered under any of the previously formed Companies Act."

Thus, a company may be defined as a legal and invisible artificial person, incorporated under an association of persons having an independent, separate legal entity along with perpetual succession and common seal, whose liability is ordinarily limited, the capital is divided into transferable shares, held by shareholders in order to earn profit.

Characteristics of a Joint Stock Company

(1) *Legal formation:* No single individual or a group of individuals can start a business and call it a joint stock company. A joint stock company comes into existence only when it has been registered after completion of all the formalities required by the Indian Companies Act, 1956.

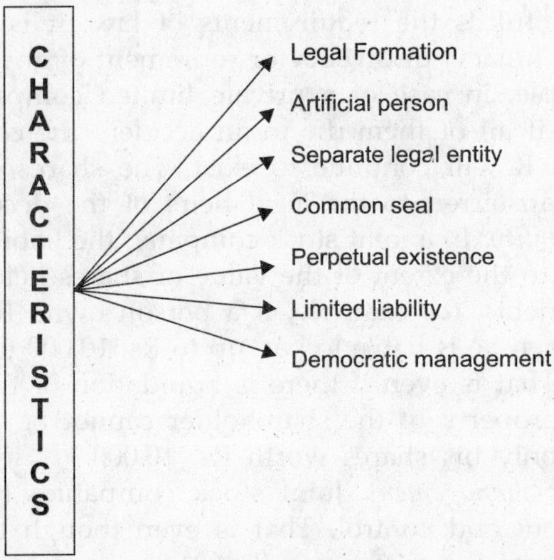

(2) *Artificial person:* Just like an individual who takes birth, grows, enters into relationship and dies, a joint stock company takes birth, enters into relationship and dies. However, it is called an artificial person as its birth, and existence and death are regulated by law and it does not possess physical attributes like that of a normal person.

(3) *Separate legal entity:* Being an artificial person, a joint stock company has its own separate existence independent of its members. It means that a joint stock company can own property, enter into contracts and conduct any lawful business in its own name. It can sue and can be sued by others in the court of law. The shareholders are not the owners of the property owned by the company. Also, the shareholders cannot be held responsible for the acts of the company.

(4) *Common seal:* A joint stock company has a seal, which is used while dealing with others or entering into contracts, with outsiders. It is called a common seal as it can be used by any officer at any level of the organization working on behalf of the company. Any document, on which the company's seal is put and is duly signed by any official of the company, becomes binding on the company. For example, a purchase manager may enter into a contract for buying raw materials from a supplier. Once the contract paper is sealed and signed by the purchase manager, it becomes valid. The purchase manager may leave the company thereafter or may be removed from the job or may have taken a wrong decision, yet for all purposes the contract is valid till a new contract is made or the existing contract expires.

(5) *Perpetual existence:* A joint stock company continues to exist as long as it fulfils the requirements of law. It is not affected by the death, lunacy, insolvency or retirement of any of its members. For example, in case of a private limited company having four members, if all of them die in an accident the company will not be closed. It will continue to exist. The shares of the company will be transferred to the legal heirs of the deceased members.

(6) *Limited liability:* In a joint stock company, the liability of a member is limited to the extent of the value of shares held by him. While repaying debts, for example, if a person owns 1000 share of Rs. 10 each, then he is liable to pay up to Rs. 10,000 towards payment of debts. That is even if there is liquidation of the company, the personal property of the shareholder cannot be attached and he will lose only his shares worth Rs. 10,000.

(7) *Democratic management:* Joint stock companies have democratic management and control. That is even though the shareholders are owners of the company, all of them cannot participate in the management of the company. Normally, the shareholders elect representatives from among themselves known as "Directors" to manage the affairs of the company.

Types of Companies

We find a variety of companies in our country. The formation liability, management and ownership of all companies differ from each other. Let us classify the different types of companies on the basis of their ownership and nationality. Accordingly, we have three types of companies – Private Limited, Public Limited, and Government Companies or the basis of ownership and two types of companies – Indian and Foreign, on the basis of nationality.

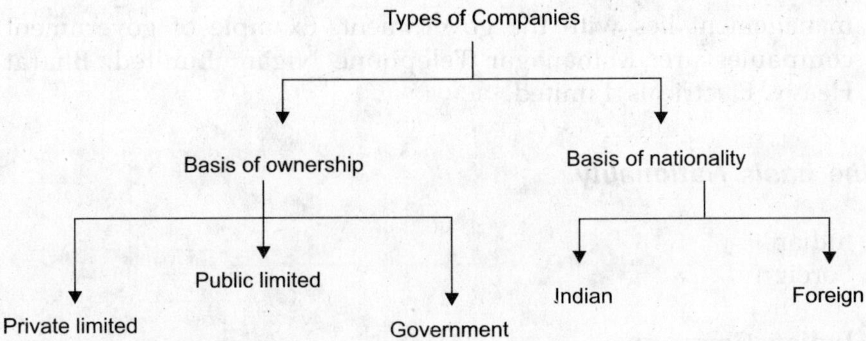

On the basis of ownership

(i) Private Limited
(ii) Public Limited
(iii) Government

(i) Private Limited Company

These companies can be formed by at least two individuals having minimum paid-up capital of not less than rupees one lakh. As per the Companies Act, 1956 the total membership of these companies cannot exceed 50. The shares allotted to its members are also not freely transferable between them. These companies are not allowed to raise money from the public through open invitation. They are required to use "Private Limited" after their names. The examples of such companies are Combined Marketing Services Private Limited, Indian Publishers and Distributors Private Limited, Oricom Systems Private Limited, etc.

(ii) Public Limited Company

A minimum of seven members are required to form a public limited company. It must have minimum paid up capital of Rs. 5 lakh. There is no restriction on maximum number of members. The shares allotted to the members are freely transferable. These companies can raise funds from general public through open invitation by selling its shares or accepting fixed deposits. These companies are required to write either 'Public Limited' or 'Limited' after their names – examples of such companies are Steel Authority of India Limited, etc.

(iii) Government Company

According to Sec. 617 of the Act and it means the companies the Government (either state or central govt. or both) holds a majority share capital, i.e., not less than 51%. However, companies having less than 51% shares holding by the government can also be called government companies provided control and management lies with the government. Example of government companies are: Mahanagar Telephone Nigam Limited, Bharat Heavy Electricals Limited.

On the basis Nationality

(i) Indian
(ii) Foreign

(i) Indian Company

A company having business operations in India and registered under the Indian Companies Act, 1956 is called Indian Company. An Indian Company may be formed as a Public Limited, Private Limited or Government Company.

(ii) Foreign Company

According to Sec. 591 of the Act, a Foreign Company is a company formed and registered outside India having business operations in India.

Company Limited by Guarantee

It is defined in Section 12(2)(b) of the Act and it means a company having the liability of its members limited by the memorandum to such amount as the member may respectively undertake by the memorandum to contribute to the assets of the company in the event of its being wound-up. Such company could be a "Company limited by guarantee and not having share capital" or a "Company limited by guarantee and having a share capital".

Unlimited Company

It is defined in Section 12(2)(c) of the Act and it means a company not having any limit on the liability to its numbers. The liability of a number extends to the whole amount of company debts and liabilities but the member will be entitled to claim contribution from other members.

Producer Company

It is defined in Section 581 A of the Act and it means a body corporate having objects or activities specified in Section 581 D and registered producer company under the Act.

The objects of the producer company shall relate to all or any of the following matters, namely,

(1) Production harvesting, procurement, grading, pooling, handling, marketing, selling of primary produce of the members or import of goods on service for their benefit. Provided that company may carry or any of the activities specified in the clause either by itself or through others institution.
(2) Processing including preserving, dying, distilling, brewing, canning, packaging of produce of its members.
(3) Manufacture, sale or supply of machinery, equipment or consumables mainly to its members.
(4) Providing education on the mutual assistance principles to its members and others.
(5) Rendering technical services, consultancy services, training, research and development and all other activities for the production of the interest of its members.
(6) Insurance of producers on their primary produce.

Holding Company

A holding company is a company or firm that owns other companies outstanding stock. The later usually refers to a company which does not produce goods or services itself, rather its purpose is to own shares of other companies. Holding companies allow the reduction of risk for the owners and can allow the ownership and control of a number of different companies.

Subsidiary Company

A company controlled by another company. A company is deemed to be a subsidiary of another if (but only if) that:

(1) Is a member of it and controls the composition of its board of directors or
(2) Holds more than half in nominal value of its equity share capital or
(3) The first mentioned company is a subsidiary of any company which is that other subsidiary.

Comparison between Private Limited Company and Public Limited Company

(1) *Minimum number of members:* The minimum number of members to constitute a private company is two but a public company cannot be formed unless there are at least seven members.

(2) *Maximum number of members:* The maximum number of members in case of private company is fifty but there is no maximum limit of members for a public company. It can have members equal to the number of shares issued by it.

(3) *Issue of prospectus:* A private company cannot invite public to subscribe to its shares or debentures by issue of prospectus for inviting public to subscribe to its shares or debentures. Membership of a private company is restricted to friends because it cannot invite public to subscribe to its shares.

(4) *Transfer of shares:* The transfer of shares is generally restricted by the articles of association of a private company. But the shares of public company are freely transferable and subscribe to its shares.

(5) *Commencement of business:* A private company can allot shares and commence business after getting the certificate of incorporation from the Registrar of Companies. But public limited company cannot allot shares unless it has collected minimum subscription and has received at least 5% of the nominal amount of share capital in cash on application. It can commence business only after getting the certificate of commencement of business. As per recent guidelines issued by Central Government, the minimum subscription in case of public rights issue of shares or debentures, has been fixed to 90% of the entire issue. Such subscription must be raised within 90 days of the close of the issue.

(6) *Number of directors:* A private limited company must have at least two directors whereas a public limited company is required to have at least three directors.

(7) *Quorum for meetings:* The quorum for a meeting of a private company is two while five members constitute a quorum in case of public company.

(8) *Use of the word limited:* In case of a private company, the word 'Private Limited' must be used at the end of the name of a company. But the word 'limited' is used at the end of the name of public company.

(9) *Legal formalities:* A private limited company is required to observe less number of legal formalities as compared to a public company. For example, a private company is not required to call a statutory meeting and file a statutory report to the Registrar of Companies. A private company need to send the list of directors, a director's consent to acts as such, a director's contract to take up qualifications shares, etc. to the Registrar of Companies.

(10) *Restriction regarding managerial remuneration:* Public limited company cannot pay managerial remuneration in any financial year more than 11% of the net profits of the company for the financial year. But no such restriction applies in case of a private limited company.

Advantages of Joint Stock Company

There are many advantages which the company form of business organization enjoys over other forms of business organization.

(1) *Huge financial resources:* A company can collect large sum of money from large number of shareholders. There is no limit on the number of shareholders in a public company. Since its capital is divided into shares of small value even a person of small means can contribute to its capital by simply purchasing its shares. It facilitates the mobilization of saving of millions for the productive purposes. In addition, a company can borrow from banks to a large extent and also issue debentures to public.

(2) *Limited liability:* The liability of shareholders in a company is limited to the face value of the shares they have purchased. The limited liability encourages many people to invest in shares of joint stock companies. If the funds of a company are insufficient to satisfy the claims of the creditors no member can be called to pay anything more than the value of shares held by them.

(3) *Perpetual existence:* Due to its separate legal entity, it has perpetual existence. The life of the company is not dependent on the death of its owners/directors. The stability of business is of great importance to the society as well as to the nation.

(4) *Transferability of shares:* The shares of a public company are freely transferable. This transferability of shares brings about liquidity of investment. It encourages many people to invest. It also helps a company in tapping more resources.

(5) *Diffusion of risk:* In sole partnership and in partnership business, the risk is shared by a few persons. But in company, the number of shareholders is large. So, many persons share risk. Therefore, the burden of risk upon any individual is not huge. This attracts many investors and enables companies to take up new ventures.

(6) *Efficient management:* In company ownership is separate from management. A company has enough resources to utilize the services of experts and managers who are highly specialized in different fields of management. It can attract talented persons by offering them higher salaries and better carrier opportunities. The efficient management helps the company to take balanced decisions and can direct the affairs of the company in the best possible manner. It also helps to expand and diversify the activities of the company.

(7) *Economics of large-scale production:* Large-scale production of modern days is the result of company form of organization. This results in economics in production, purchase, marketing and management. These economics help company to provide quality

goods at lower cost to the consumers.

(8) *Democratic management:* The company is managed by the elected representatives of shareholders called the 'Director'. Directors are responsible and accountable to the general body of shareholders. Decisions are taken by a majority of votes completely based upon democratic principles. This prevents in mismanagement of a company.

(9) *Public confidence:* A company enjoys a greater public confidence and reputation in the market due to legal control, publicity of accounts and perpetual existence. Audit of joint stock company is compulsory. A company's financial accounts and statements are published, circulated and are open to public inspection. Therefore, people have enough faith in it. So, it can get loan from different financial institutions.

(10) *Social importance:* The company provides opportunity to mobilize scattered saving of the community. It also creates employment opportunities. Due to large-scale production consumers get cheaper goods. The society is supplied with enough quantity of goods. Government gets income in the form of taxes.

Disadvantages

(1) *Difficulty in formation:* A company is not easy to form and establish. A number of persons should be ready to associate for getting a company incorporated. It requires lot of legal formalities to be performed. The shares will have to be sold during the prescribed time. It is both expensive and risky.

(2) *Lack of secrecy:* A company has to observe many legal formalities. Most of the business activities are decided through meetings. Profit and loss accounts and balance sheet are required to be published. So, trade secrets cannot be maintained.

(3) *Delay in decisions:* In company, decision-making process is time consuming. All important decisions are made by either Board of Directors or by General Annual Meetings. So, many opportunities may be lost due to delay in decision-making.

(4) *Separation of ownership and management:* A company is owned by shareholders but, managed by directors. The shareholders play an insignificant role in the working of the company. Though directors are owners of some qualification shares only, yet the impact of their activities are to be borne by all shareholders. The profit of the company belongs to shareholders and the Board of Directors is paid only a commission. There is no direct relationship between efforts and rewards. So, the management

does not take personal interest in the working of company. Hence, they may work against the interest of vast majority of shareholders.

(5) *Speculation in shares:* A joint stock company facilitates speculation in the shares at stock exchanges. It has been found that even the directors and the managers of the company indulge in manipulating the value of shares to their advantage. When they want to purchase the shares they lower the rate of dividend and when they want to dispose of the shares they declare dividends at a higher rate.

(6) *Oligarchic management:* The shareholders who are the real owners do not have much influence in the management. A handful of shareholders, which also manage the affairs of the company have control over it. Theoretically, the company is democratic but in practice it is mostly a case of oligarchy (rule by few). A few persons hold power and control and try to exploit the majority. Thus, it does not promote the interest of the shareholders in general.

(7) *Excessive regulation:* A company has to observe excessive regulations imposed by the law of the company. The excessive regulations are made with a view to protect the interest of the shareholders and its public but in practice they put obstacles in their normal and effective working. A lot of precious time, efforts and financial resources are wasted in complying with statutory requirements.

(8) *Conflict of interest:* In a company there are many parties whose interest may clash and the result may be conflict of interests. The management, the shareholders, the employees, the creditors and the government may have their own individual interests. Thus, a permanent type of conflict of interest may continue to exist in the companies. These conflicts generally lead inefficiency in the management and reduce employees' morale.

(9) *Neglect of minority:* All major issues in company are decided by the shareholders having majority of them. Majority always dominates over the minority group whose interests are never represented in the management. The Company Act provides measures against oppression of minority, but these measures are not very effective.

Formation of a Company

Company formation is the process of incorporation of a business. It is also referred to as company registration. Here, the stages involved in its formation of a joint stock company and the important documents that regulate the functioning of company are stated.

Stages in the Formation of a Joint Stock Company

It is easy to establish a sole proprietorship business or a partnership firm as there are a few regulations to meet. But for the establishment of a company, a lot of formalities are to be complied with. The registration of a company is mandatory before starting its operations. The formation of a company, right from the origin of idea to establish a company goes through four different stages, like:

Stage I Promotion
Sage II Incorporation
Stage III Raising of Capital
Stage IV Commencement of Business

Stage I: Promotion

Promotion of business simply refers to all those activities that are required to be undertaken to establish a new business unit for manufacturing or distribution of any product or provide any service to the people. It starts with conceiving an idea of business or discover an opportunity for doing a business, assess its feasibility and then take the necessary steps to launch the business unit. This involves ascertaining as to whether all the basic requirements such as land, building, raw material, machine, equipment, etc. are available or not. If they are available, one can assemble them, arrange the necessary funds and set up the business unit to give shape to the initial idea of establishing the business. The whole process is called 'promotion' and the person who does it, is called the 'promoter'.

Role and Importance of Promoter

A promoter can be defined as a person and group of persons who conceive the idea of setting up a new business, assess its feasibility and take necessary steps to arrange the basic requirements and establish a business unit say, a company and put it into operation. Promoter plays a pivotal role in the promotion of a company. He conceives the idea of business enterprise, analyses its prospects, works out of a tentative scheme of organization, brings together the requisite men, material, machines, and money and starts the enterprise.

Formation of A Joint Stock Company

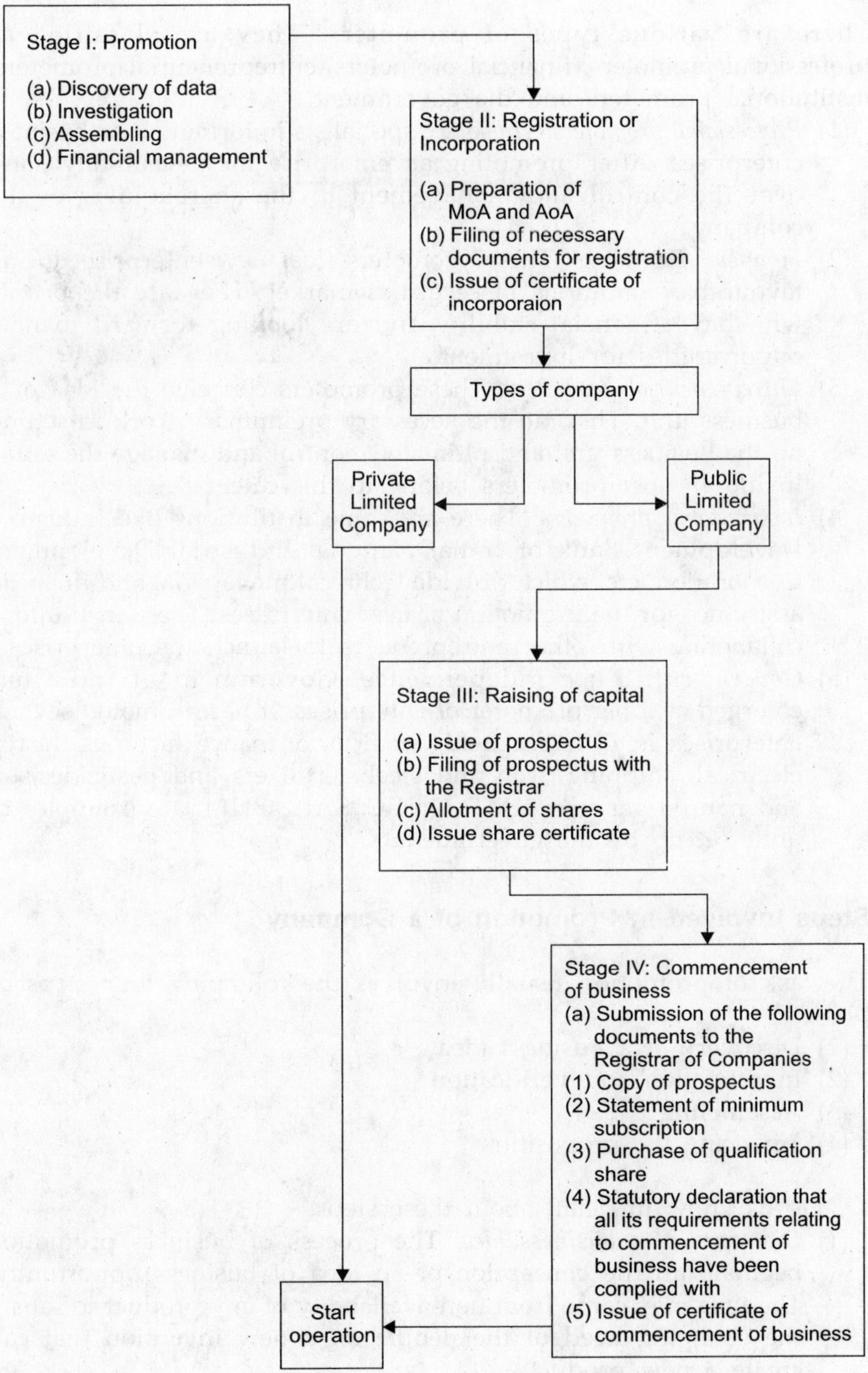

Types of Promoters

There are various types of promoters. They are classified as professional promoters, financial promoters, entrepreneurial promoters, institutional promoters and the government.

(1) *Professional promoters:* These are specialists in forming new business enterprises. After promoting an enterprise they eventually hand over the control and management to the shareholders of the company.

(2) *Financial Promoters:* These promoters float new enterprise during favourable conditions in securities market. They are the people who have financial stability and are looking forward to new opportunities for investment.

(3) *Entrepreneurial promoters:* These promoters conceive the idea of a business unit. They do the necessary preliminary work in setting up the business unit and ultimately control and manage the same. In India, most promoters belong to this category.

(4) *Institutional promoters:* There are some institutions like Industrial Development Bank of India, National Industrial Development Corporation, etc. which provide technical managerial and financial assistance for the promotion of new enterprises. These institutions collaborate with other entrepreneurs to launch the enterprises.

(5) *Government:* Since independence, Government of India has emerged as a big promoter of enterprises. It has promoted several enterprises in different fields such as ordnance factories, heavy electrical, shipping, iron and steel, fertilizers and pesticides, oil and natural gas, etc. HMT, ONGC, SAIL, BHEL are examples of units set up by the government.

Steps Involved in Promotion of a Company

The task of promotion usually involves the following four steps or phases:

(1) Discovery of a business idea
(2) Investigation and verification
(3) Assembling
(4) Financing the proposition

Let us know in detail about these steps:

(1) *Discovery of a business idea:* The process of business promotion begins with the conception of an idea of business opportunity. The idea may come from non-availability of any product to satisfy the changing need of the people on a new invention that can create a new product.

For example, during early 1940s there was no 'Walkman'. The marketing executive of an electronic company found people busy in hearing music holding a big radio on their shoulders while travelling. This particular scene perturbed the marketing executive and he thought how nice would it be if the radio could be reduced to a very small size which can be kept in pocket and a wire be connected to the ear. The idea gave birth to the new product 'Walkman".

(2) *Investigation and verification:* Once the idea has been conceived a thorough investigation is made to establish the soundness of the proposition taking into consideration its technical feasibility and commercial viability. As in the case of 'Walkman' if there was no technology by which the size of the radio to the ear could be reduced to small size or no technology to transmit the sound from the radio to the ear through earphone, the proposition of producing the "Walkman" would have been impossible. Similarly, if technology is available but the cost involved in making a "Walkman" would be so high that no customer could be able to purchase it, or the demand is too limited and the return on the investment is low, the idea is not considered commercially viable. All these investigations, technical feasibility, commercial viability, and profitability are presented in the report called 'project report' or 'feasibility report'. This feasibility report is the primary or basic document that helps in procuring licences and arrange the necessary finance from financial institutions and other investors.

(3) *Assembling:* Once the promoter is convinced of the feasibility and profitability of the proposition he takes steps in assembling or making arrangements for all the necessary requirements such as land, building, machinery, tools, capital, etc. Decision is also to be made regarding size, location and layout, etc. for the plant, and make contracts with suppliers for raw materials, enter into agreement with the dealers to purchase equipment, make agreement with bankers to finance and take initial steps for the setting up of a company.

(4) *Financing the proposition:* At this stage financial plans are prepared with respect to the amount of capital required, the nature of capital structure, i.e., the proportion of capital to be raised from owner's fund and that from borrowing from banks and others, and how and when to raise the share capital from the general public. Agreements are made with merchant bankers, underwriters and stock brokers who are to assist the capital issue, and so on.

Stage II: Incorporation

A sole proprietorship or partnership firm can be formed to carry out its business even without any registration. But a company cannot be formed or permitted to run its business without registration. In fact, a company comes into existence only when it is registered with the 'Registrar of Companies'. For this purpose, the promoter has to take the following steps:

(a) *Approval of name:* It has to be ensured that the name selected for the company does not match with the name of any other company. For this, the promoter has to fill in a "Name Availability Form" and submit it to the Registrar of Companies along with necessary fees. The name must include the words 'Limited' or 'Private Limited' at the end. Once it is approved, the promoter can proceed with other formalities for the incorporation of the company.

(b) *Filing of documents:* After getting the name approved the promoter makes an application to the Registrar of Companies of the state in which the registered office of the company is to be situated for registration of the company. The application of registration must be accompanied by the following document:

(i) Memorandum of Association (MOA): It defines the objectives of the company and states about the range of activities or operation. It must be duly stamped, signed and witnessed.

(ii) Articles of Association (AoA): It combines the rules and regulations regarding the internal management of the company. It must be properly stamped, duly signed by the signatories to the Memorandum of Association and witnessed.

(iii) A list of persons who have agreed to become directors with their addresses, etc.

(iv) Written consent of the proposed directors to act in that capacity, duly signed by each director.

(v) The notice about the exact address of the registered office of the company. It may, however, to be filed within 30 days of incorporation or registration.

(vi) A copy of the name approval letter received from the Registrar of Companies.

(vii) A statutory declaration that all the legal requirements of the Companies Act in regard to incorporation have been complied with.

(c) Payment of filing and registration fees along with the above document, necessary filing fees at the prescribed rates are also to be paid. The Registrar will scrutinize all the documents and if he finds them in order, he will issue a certificate of incorporation. The moment the certificate is issued, the company comes into existence. So, this certificate may be called the 'Birth Certificate of a Joint Stock Company'.

Stage III: Raising of Capital or Subscription of Capital

After the company is incorporated the next stage is to raise the necessary capital. In case, if a private limited company, the share capital has to be raised from the public. This involves the following:

(1) Preparation of a draft prospectus and get it inspected (vetted) by SEBI to ensure that all information given in the prospectus fully complies with the guidelines laid down by SEBI in this regard.

(2) Filing a copy of the prospectus with the Registrar of Companies.

(3) Issue of prospectus to the public by notifying in a newspaper and inviting public to apply for shares as prescribed in the prospectus.

(4) If the minimum subscription has been received, shares should be allotted to the applicants as per SEBI guidelines and a file return of allotment with the Registrar of Companies.

(5) Listing of shares in a recognized Stock Exchange so that the shares can be traded there. Preferably consent of a stock exchange for listing should be obtained before the issueing of the prospectus.

Stage IV: Commencement of Business

In case of a private limited company, it can immediately start its business as soon as it is registered. However, in case of public limited company a certificate, known as "Certificate of Commencement of Business", must be obtained from the Registrar of Companies before starting its operations. Far this purpose, it has to file a statement with the following declarations to the Registrar of Companies.

(a) That a prospectus has been filed with the Registrar of Companies.

(b) That the shares have been allotted up to the amount of the minimum subscription.

(c) That the directors have taken up or purchased the minimum number of shares required to qualify themselves to be director.

(d) That no money is liable to become refundable to the applicants by reason of failures to obtain permission far shares to be traded in a recognized stock exchange.

(e) A statutory declaration by a director on the secretary of the company stating that the requirement relating to the commencement of business have been duly complied with the Registrar of Companies will scrutinise all these documents and if he is satisfied that the process of securing the minimum prescribed capital has been honestly and efficiently followed and the minimum prescribed capital has been obtained from the public then he shall issue a certificate of commencement of business.

POINTS TO REMEMBER

Joint Stock Company	:	According to Indian Companies Act, 1956. Joint Stock Company is defined as an artificial person in the eyes of law, having a separate legal entity with a perpetual existence and a common seal.

Characteristic features of Joint Stock Company

All the features must be explained for section 'B' or section 'C' questions. viz.,

(a) Legal formation
(b) Artificial person
(c) Separate legal entity
(d) Common seal
(e) Perpetual existence
(f) Limited liabilities
(g) Democratic management

Types of Companies

(a) On the basis of ownership
  (i) Private companies
  (ii) Public companies
  (iii) Government companies
(b) On the basis of nationality
  (i) Indian companies
  (ii) Foreign companies

Difference between private limited company and public limited company.

		Private company	Public company
1.	Minimum number of members	Two	Seven
2.	Maximum number of members	50	Unlimited
3.	Issues of prospectus	General public cannot subscribe to the capital	General public can contribute to the capital
4.	Transfer of shares	Restricted	Can be traded in Stock Exchange
5.	Comencent of business	Can start the business immediately after certificate of incorporation	Can start the business immediately after obtaining certificate of commencement of business
6.	Number of directors	Two	Three
7.	Quorum for meeting	Two	Five
8.	Use of the word limited	Pvt. limited term used at the end of the name of the company	Limited term is used at the end of the name of the company
9.	Number of legal formalities	Very less	Large number

Government company : More than 51% of the shares of these companies are held by government.

Companies limited by guarantee : In the event of loss of these companies, the promoter's liabilities will be extended to the agreed/guaranteed amount.

Unlimited company : Liability of the members of these companies are unlimited to the extent of clearing the debt of the company.

Producing company : These are the companies which engage themselves in growing or producing some products or services which are demanded in the market.

Holding company : A company or firm that owns other companies outstanding stock.

Subsidiary company : It is a company in which 51% of the shares are held by some other company.

Formation of a joint stock company

(i) Promotion
(ii) Incorporation
(iii) Raising of share capital
(iv) Commencement of business

Types of Promoters

(1) Professional promoters
(2) Financial promoters
(3) Entrepreneurial promoters
(4) Institutional promoters
(5) Government

QUESTION BANK

SECTION A (Objective type) (2 marks)

(1) What is a Joint Stock Company?
(2) Mention any two characteristic features of a Joint Stock Company.
(3) What is meant by private limited company?
(4) What is meant by public limited company?
(5) What is meant by Government Company?
(6) What is meant by Indian company?
(7) What is meant by foreign company?
(8) What is a holding company?
(9) What is a subsidiary company?
(10) Who is a professional promoter?
(11) Who is a financial promoter?
(12) What is meant by Memorandum of Association?

SECTION B (Analytical or descriptive types)

(1) Analyze the characteristics of a Joint Stock Company.
(2) Analyze the differences between private limited company and public limited company.
(3) Write a brief note on:
   (a) Memorandum of Association.
   (b) Articles of Association.

SECTION C (Essay type questions)

(1) Explain the advantages and disadvantages of a Joint Stock Company.
(2) Explain the different stages involved in the formation of a Joint Stock Company.

Unit 4
Business Environment

Meaning of Business Environment – Features – Importance – Components of Business Environment – Micro – Macro Environment – Economic Environment – Political Environment – Socio-cultural Environment – Technological Environment – Legal Environment – Provision of the Constitutation – Natural Environment – Demographical Environment – International Environment.

LEARNING OBJECTIVE

This chapter takes the reader to understand the environmental issues essentially needed to start a business. Business organizations are the part and parcel of the society; hence, issues discussed in this chapter offer the reader all ingredients to take the decisions to start a business firm. Understanding the environment within which the business has to operate is very important for running a business unit successfully at any place. Because the environmental factors influence almost every aspect of business, be its nature, its location, the price of products, the distribution system, or the policies. Hence, it is important to learn about the various components of the business environment, which consists of legal aspects, the economic aspects, the socio-cultural aspects, the political framework, and the technological aspects, etc. In this chapter, we shall learn about the concepts of business environment, its nature and significance and the various components of the environment.

4

Business Environment

MEANING OF BUSINESS ENVIRONMENT

Environment of a business means the external forces influencing the business decisions. They can be forces of economic, social, political and technological. These forces are beyond the control of the business. The business can do little to change them. As stated earlier, the success of every business depends on adapting itself to the environment within which it functions. For example, when there is a change in the government policies, the business has to make the necessary changes to adapt itself to the new policies. Similarly, a change in the technology may render the existing products obsolete. We have seen that the introduction of computer has replaced the typewriters; the colour television has made the black and white television out of fashion. Again a change in the fashion or customers' taste may shift the demand in the market for a particular product, e.g., the demand for jeans reduced the sale of other traditional wear. All these aspects are external factors that are beyond the control of the business. So the business units must have to adapt themselves to this kind of changes, in order to survive and succeed in business. Hence, it is necessary to have a clear understanding of the concepts of business environment and the nature of its various components. The term 'business environment' connotes external forces, factors and institutions that are beyond the control of the business and they affect the functioning of a business enterprise. These include customers, competitors, suppliers, government and the social, political, legal and technological factors, etc. While some of these factors/forces may have direct influence over the business firms, others may operate indirectly. Thus, business environment may be defined as the total surroundings, which have a direct or indirect bearing on the functioning of business. It may also be defined as the set of external factors, such as economic factors, social factors, political and legal

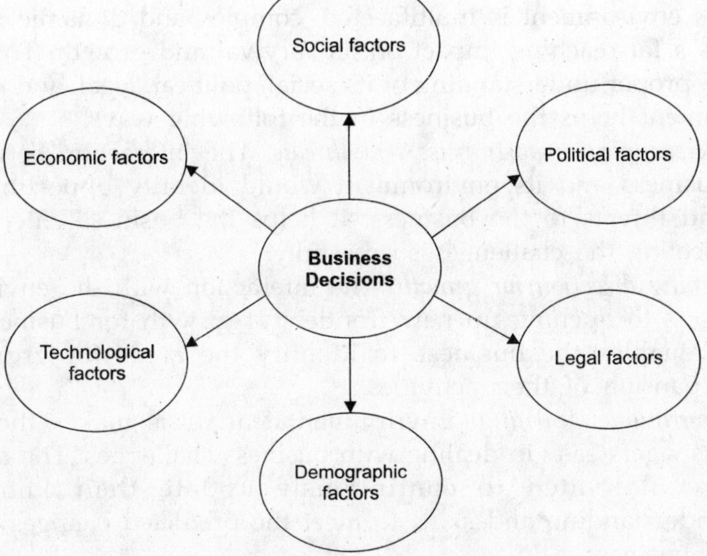

factors, and demographic factors, technical factors, etc. which are uncontrollable in nature and affect the business decisions of a firm.

FEATURES OF BUSINESS ENVIRONMENT

On the basis of the above discussion the features of business environment can be summarized as followed.

(1) Business environment is the sum total of all factors external to the business firm and that greatly influence their functioning.
(2) It covers customers, competitors, suppliers, government and the social, cultural, political, technological and legal conditions.
(3) The business environment is dynamic in nature, that means, it keeps on changing.
(4) The changes in the business environment are unpredictable. It is difficult to predict the exact nature of happenings and the changes in economic and social environment.
(5) Business environment differs from place to place, region to region and country to country. Political conditions in India differ from those in Pakistan. Trader and values cherished by people in India and China vary considerably.

IMPORTANCE OF BUSINESS ENVIRONMENT

There is a close and continuous interaction between the business and its environment. This interaction helps in strengthening the business firm and using its resources more effectively. As stated above, the business environment is multifaceted, complex and dynamic in nature and has a far-reaching impact on its survival and growth. To be more specific, proper understanding of its social, political, legal, and economic environment helps the business in the following ways:

(1) *Determining opportunities and threats:* The interaction between the business and its environment would identify opportunities for and threats to the business. It helps the business enterprise for meeting the challenges successfully.

(2) *Giving direction for growth:* The interaction with the environment leads to opening up new frontiers of growth for business firms. It enables the business to identify the areas for growth and expansion of their activities.

(3) *Continuous learning:* Environmental analysis makes the task of managers easy in dealing with business challenges. The managers are motivated to continuously update their knowledge, understanding and skills to meet the predicted changes in realm of business.

(4) *Image building:* Environmental understanding helps the business organizations in improving their image by showing their sensitivity to the environment within which they are working. For example, in view of the shortage of power many companies have set up Captive Power Plants (CPP) in their factories to meet their own requirements of power.

(5) *Meeting competition:* It helps the firms to analyze the competitor's strategy and formulate their own accordingly.

(6) *Identifying firm's strengths and weaknesses:* Business environment helps to identify the strengths and weaknesses in view of the technological and global development.

(7) *Keeping business flexible and dynamic:* Study of business environment is needed for keeping business flexible and dynamic as per the changes in the environmental forces. This will enable the development of business organization.

(8) *Understanding the future prospects and problems:* Business environment enables to understand future problems and prospects of business in advance. This enables the organization to be more research oriented to make positive contributions toward the organizational goals and enables them to face the problems boldly and also take its benefit of favourable situations.

(9) *Making the business socially acceptable:* Environment study enables the businessmen to expand the business and also make it acceptable to different social groups. Business organizations can make positive contribution for maintaining ecological balance by studying social environment.

(10) *Ensures optimum utilization of resources:* The study of business environment is needed as it ensures optimum use of resources available. For this, the study of economic and technological environment enables the organization to take full benefit of government polices, concessions provided and technological developments and so on.

(11) *Ensures survival and growth:* Business environment informs about suitable changes to be effected in business policies. This helps the business organization to grow and prosper.

(12) *Maintaining adaptability to changes:* Business environment guides the organization about socio-economic changes and the organization must accordingly adapt these changes. This enables the business, organization to survive for a longer period.

COMPONENTS OF BUSINESS ENVIRONMENT

Business environment has two components:

(a) Internal environment
(b) External environment

(a) Internal Environment

Internal environment refers to environment within the organization. It includes internal factors of the business which can be controlled by business. It includes objectives of business managerial policies, management and employees of the organization, labour management relationship, brand image and corporate image, working conditions in the organization, technological and research and development capabilities. Internal environment includes 5 M's i.e., men, materials, machinery, management available with business. These components are usually within the control of business.

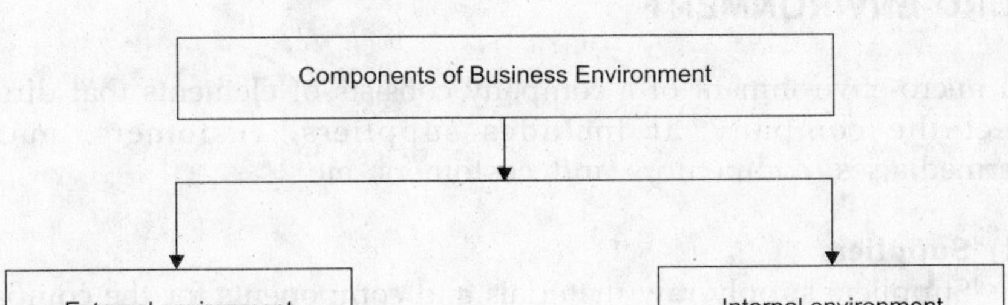

(b) External Environment

External environment refers to external aspects of the surroundings of business enterprise which have influence on the functioning of business. These factors are beyond the control of business. External environment includes factors outside the firm which can provide opportunities or pose threats to the firm.

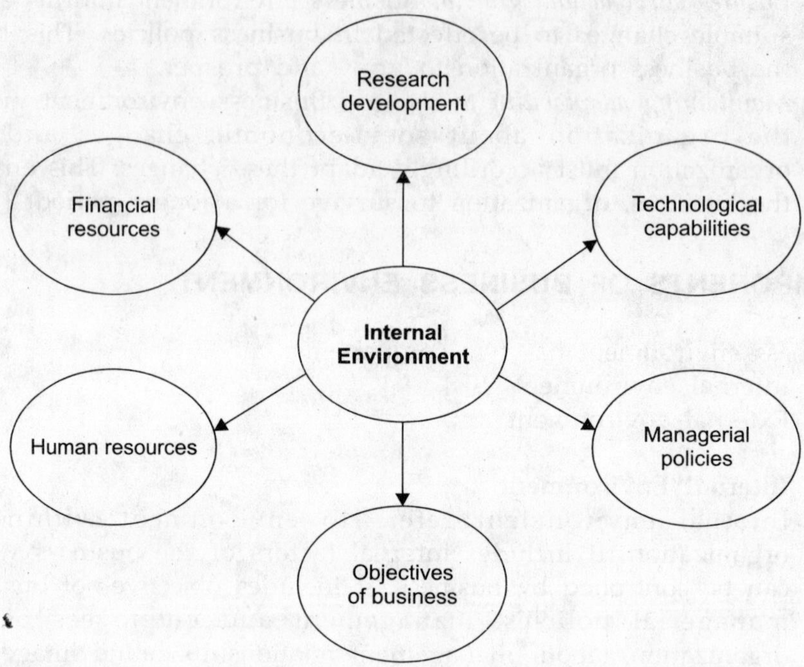

External environment has two types:

(i) Micro-environment

(ii) Macro-environment

MICRO-ENVIRONMENT

The micro-environment of a company consists of elements that directly affect the company. It includes suppliers, customers, market intermediaries, competitors and customers, etc.

(1) Suppliers

Suppliers supply raw materials and components for the company. Every business requires the suppliers. If our supplier is reliable, our business swill run smoothly, if our supplier is not reliable, we have to maintain high inventories.

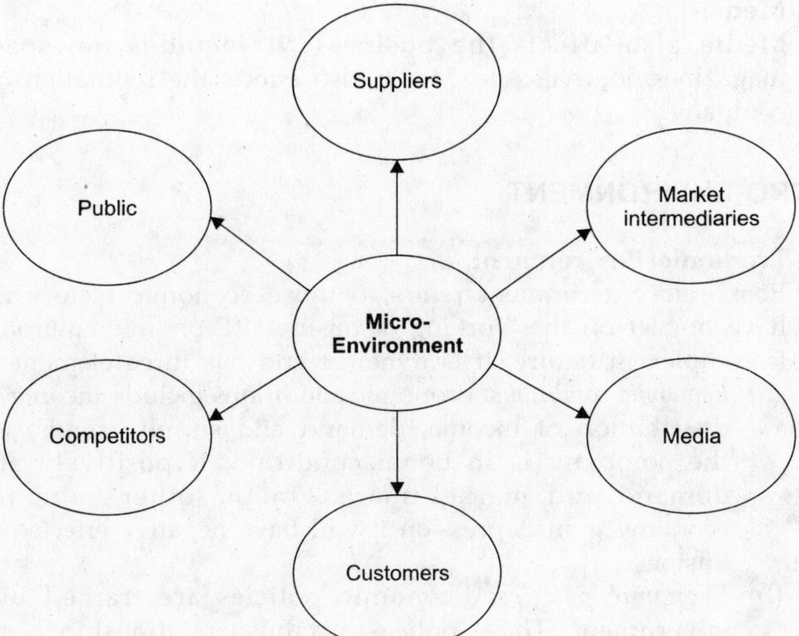

(2) Customer

Customer is the central point of any business. The success of a business organization depends upon the customers, their needs, tastes, etc. Nowadays, the competition is growing so fast that it is essential to satisfy the customer. For attracting new customers companies conduct consumer research, provide after-sales services, etc.

(3) Market intermediaries

Market intermediaries include agents and brokers who help the company to find customers. It is a link between the company and the consumer. Market intermediaries help the company to promote, sell and distribute its goods to final buyers. Market intermediaries include middlemen, marketing agencies, financial intermediaries, physical intermediaries, etc.

(4) Competitors

Competitors means other business units which are producing similar products or a very close substitute to the product. Nowadays competition has increased. No business unit enjoys monopoly in the market. So the business has to satisfy the customer for it success in the market.

(5) Public

Public is a group that has actual or potential interest in the business. So public also affects the business.

(6) Media

Media also affects the business. It includes newspapers, magazines, journals, etc. Media also affects the reputation of the company.

MACRO-ENVIRONMENT

(1) Economic Environment

Economic environment refers to those economic factors which have impact on the working of business. Economic environment is complex in nature. It is dynamic and has three elements:

(a) *Economic conditions:* Economic conditions include income level, distribution of income, demand and supply trends, etc. If the company is in boom condition, it positively affects demand and market share. On the other hand if the economy is in depression it will have negative effects on the business.

(b) *Economic policies:* Economic policies are framed by the government. These policies establish relationship between business and government. The effect of these policies may be favourable or unfavourable. Some of the policies are:

(i) Industrial

(ii) Fiscal

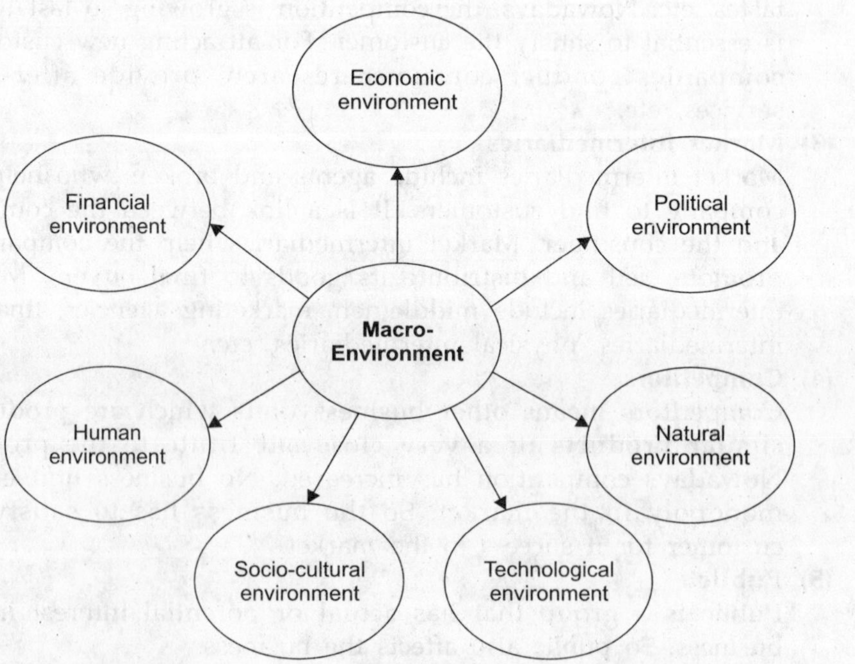

(iii) Monetary
(iv) Foreign investment
(v) Export-import (EXIM).

(c) *Economic system:* Different economic systems prevail in different countries. These systems affect the business. The economic systems includes capitalism, socialism and mixed economies. The world economy is primarily governed by three types of economic systems i.e.,:
(1) Capitalist economy
(2) Socialist economy
(3) Mixed economy

India follows the mixed economy system which implies co-existence of public sector and private sector.

As an introduction to the analysis of the business environment in any economy, you may consider the three basic propositions given below:

1. Business is an economic activity.
2. A business firm is an economic unit.
3. Business decision-making is an economic process.

These propositions may be examined separately or jointly to justify the study of the economic environment of business in any country.

Business is an economic activity

An economic activity involves the task of adjusting the means (resources) to the ends (targets), or the ends to the means. An economic activity may assume different forms such as consumption, production, distribution, and exchange. The nature of business differs depending upon the form of economic activity being undertaken and organized. The point to be noted is that each business has a target to achieve, and for this purpose each business has some resources at its disposal. Sometimes the target has to be matched with the given resources, and sometimes the resources have to be matched with the given target. Either way, the task of business is to optimize the outcome of economic activities.

A business firm is an economic unit

A business firm is essentially a transformation unit. It transforms input into output of goods or services, or a combination of both. The nature of input requirements and the type of output flows are determined by the size, structure, location and efficiency of the business firm under consideration. Business firms may be of different sizes and forms. They may undertake different types of activities such as mining, manufacturing, farming, trading, transporting, banding etc. The motivational objective underlying all these activities is the same viz., profit maximization in the long run. Profit is essentially "a surplus value"- the value of outputs in excess of the values of inputs or the surplus of revenue over the cost. A business firm undertakes the transformational progress to generate this "surplus value". The firm can grow further if the surplus value is productively invested. The firm, therefore, carefully plans the optimum allocation of resources (i.e., men, money, material, machines time, energy, etc.) to get optimum production. The entire process of creating, mobilization and utilization of the surplus constitutes the economic activity of the business firm.

Business decision-making is an economic process

Decision-making involves making a choice from a set of alternative courses of action. Choice is at the root of all economic activities. The question of choice and evaluation arises because of the relative scarcity of resources. If the resources had not been scarce, an unlimited amount of ends could have been met. But the situation of resources constraint is very real. A business firm thinks seriously about the optimum allocation of resources because resources are limited in supply and most resources have alternative uses. The firm, therefore, intends to get the best out of given resources or to minimize the use of resources for achieving a specific target. In other words, when "input" is the constraining factor, the firm's decision variable is the "output". And when "output" is the constraining factor, the firm's decision variable is the "input". Whatever may be the decision variable, procurement or production, distribution or sale, input or output, decision-making is invariably the process of selecting the best available alternative. That is what makes it an economic pursuit.

Since business is an economic activity, a business firm is an economic unit, and business decision-making an economic process, it is the economics environment of business which is the primary consideration in evaluating the business policies, business strategies and business tactics of a corporate entity in any national economy.

(2) Political Environment

Political environment affects the different business units. A stable and dynamic political environment is necessary for business growth. Political environment includes political stability in the country, relation of the government with other countries, welfare activities of government, centre-state relationship, views of opposition parties towards business. If the political system is stable and efficient then the business grows. In the absence of political stability long-term plans cannot be formulated. Similarly, relations of government with other countries also affect business. If a country enjoys friendly relations with other nations then it has favourable effect on foreign trade. You may be aware that Coca-Cola, a cold drink widely consumed, had to wind up operations in India in late seventies. The trade union activities also influence the operation of business enterprises. Most of the labour unions in India are aligned with various political parties. However, with competitive business environment, trade unions are now showing great maturity and have started contributing positively to the success of the business organizations through workers' participation and management. No matter how attractive the economic prospects of a particular country or region are, doing business there might prove to be financially disastrous if the host government(s) inflict(s) heavy financial penalties on a company or if unanticipated events in the political arena lead to the loss of income-generating assets. The political environment in which the firm operates (or plans to operate) will have a significant impact on a company's international marketing activities. The greater the level of involvement in a foreign market, the greater the need to monitor the political climate. Changes in government often result in changes in policy and attitudes towards foreign business. Bearing in mind that a foreign company operates in a host country at the discretion of the government concerned, the government can either encourage foreign activities by offering attractive opportunities for investment and trade, or discourage its activities by imposing restrictions such as import quotas, etc. An exporter that is continuously aware of shifts in government attitude, will be able to adapt export marketing strategies accordingly. Nearly all governments today play active roles in their countries' economies. Although evident to a greater or lesser extent in most countries, government ownership of economic activities is still prevalent in the former centrally planned economies, as well as in certain developing countries which lack a sufficiently well developed private sector to support a free market system. The implications of government ownership to a company marketing abroad might be that certain sectors of the foreign market are the exclusive preserve of government enterprise or that the company is obliged to sell directly to a state trading organization. In either case, the company's influence on the market is greatly reduced. Similarly, if an exporter is seeking to establish a subsidiary in a country where there is a high degree of state influence over the factors of production, the investor should bear in mind that marketing activities in the country concerned may be restricted and that the so-called controllable elements of the marketing mix will be less controllable. Of primary concern to an exporter should be the stability of the target country's political environment. A loss of confidence in this respect could lead to a company having to reduce its operations in the market or to withdraw from the market altogether. One of the surest indicators of political instability is a frequent change in regime. Although a change in government need not be accompanied by violence, it often heralds a change in policy towards business, particularly international business. Such a development could impact harshly a firm's long-term international marketing programme. Reflected in government's attitudes and policies towards foreign business are its ideas about how best to promote national interest in the light of the country's economic and political resources and objectives. Foreign products and investment seen to be vital to the growth and development of the economy often receive favourable treatment from the government in the form of reduced tax, exemption from quotas, etc. On the other hand, products considered by a government to be non-essential, undesirable, or a threat to local industry are frequently subjected to a variety of import restrictions such as quotas and tariffs. It is also important to be aware of the nature of the relationship between India and the foreign target market.

(3) Socio-cultural Environment

Socio-cultural environment refers to social and cultural factors which are beyond the control of business units. Such factors include attitude of people to work, family system, caste system, education system, habits, language, religion, etc. Socio-cultural environment is one of the important non-economic external components of business environment. Religion has considerable effect on business. Some religions restrict their followers, they do not allow its followers to engage in leather industry, wine making, etc. Similarly, the social environment of business also includes social factors like customer, traditions, values, beliefs, poverty, literacy, life expectancy rate, etc. The social structure and the values that a society cherishes have a considerable influence on the fractioning of business firms. For example, during festive seasons there is an increase in the demand for new clothes, sweets, fruits, flowers, etc. Due to increase in literacy rate the consumers are more cautious of quality of the products. Due to change in family composition, more nuclear families with single child concept have come up. This increases the demand for the different types of household goods. It may be noted that the consumption patterns, the dressings and living styles of people belonging to different social strata and culture vary significantly. Similarly, difference in language is another problem area at national of and international level business. The businessman must be familiar with the local language of the place where business is to be operated.

Humans essentially create their own cultural and social environment. Customs, practices and traditions for survival and development are passed down from one generation to the next. In this way, the members of a particular society become conditioned to accept certain "truths" about life around them. The increasingly competitive international business environment calls upon exporters to tailor or adapt their business approach to the culture and traditions of specific foreign markets. The inability or unwillingness to do so could become a serious obstacle to success.

The task of adjusting to a new cultural environment is probably one of the biggest challenges of export marketing. Export marketing attempts are frequently unsuccessful because the marketer – either consciously or unconsciously – makes decisions or evaluations from a frame of reference that is acceptable to his/her own culture but unacceptable in a foreign environment. Therefore, business practices which are successful in one group of countries may be entirely inappropriate in another group of countries. For example, the Marlboro Company took its famous lone cowboy advertisement to Hong Kong in the early 1960's.However, the image of the cowboy riding off in the distance by himself led the Chinese to wonder what he had done wrong.

In the context of the socio-cultural environment, there are a number of factors that you will need to consider. These are:

1. Language
2. Material culture
3. Aesthetics
4. Social organisation
5. Religious beliefs, attitudes, values, space and time

Language

Language is central to the expression of culture. Within each cultural group, the use of words reflects the lifestyle, attitudes and many of the customs of that group. Language is not only a key to understanding the group, it is the principal way of communicating within it.

A language usually defines the parameters of a particular culture. Thus if several languages are spoken within the borders of a country, that country is seen to have as many cultures. In our own country there are over 20 official languages and we have hundreds of dialects of these languages. In Canada, for instance, both English and French are spoken; in Belgium, French and Flemish; while in South Africa there are 11 official languages with a number of other African languages also spoken by the population. In addition, there are often variations within a language - different dialects, accents, pronunciations and terminology may distinguish one cultural group from another. Learning some of the subtleties of a language can assist greatly in avoiding confusion:

The importance of being able to understand other languages cannot be over-emphasised - this is particularly relevant when executives travel abroad and negotiate with people of different language groups. Because English is the predominant language of business in the western world, people with English as a home language are usually reluctant to learn foreign languages and tend to expect others to converse with them in English. In contrast, European and Far Eastern businesspersons have been willing to learn and converse in the language of their trading partners, leading inevitably to a better understanding and better rapport between the parties concerned. If exporters do not speak the language of the country they plan to visit, they should at least establish the extent to which their own language is spoken there and, if necessary, engage the services of an interpreter during discussions or negotiations.

If promotional material needs to be prepared in a foreign language, it is important to ensure that none of the meaning is lost or distorted when the information is translated. Thus, translations should be undertaken within the country concerned or at least by a native of the country in question.

Material Culture

Material culture relates to the way in which a society organises and views its economic activities. It includes the techniques and knowhow used in the creation of goods and services, the manner in which the people of the society use their capabilities, and the resulting benefits. When one refers to an 'industrialised' or a 'developing' nation, one is really referring to a material culture.

The material culture of a particular market will affect the nature and extent of demand for a product. Whereas a luxury item, such as a sophisticated piece of computer hardware, may have a ready market in a country such as France, demand for it may be non-existent in a developing country which is hampered by inadequate facilities and/or foreign exchange shortages. The material culture of a country may also necessitate modifications to the product. Electrical appliances, for example, may have to be adapted to cater for differences in voltage levels. To illustrate this: the United States operates under a system of 110V in contrast to India's 220V. Alternatively, weights and measurements may have to be converted to those applicable in the importing country (again the US uses measures such as miles, gallons and pounds, whereas most other parts of the world use the metric system - kilometres, litres and kilograms).

Material culture can also have a significant effect on the proposed marketing and distribution strategies. While highways and rail transport are the principal means of moving goods within India, China and United States, rivers and canals are used extensively in certain European countries. If the company is planning to develop a manufacturing operation in a foreign market, aspects such as the supply of raw materials, power, transportation and financing need to be investigated.

Aesthetics

A culture's aesthetics refers to its ideas concerning good taste and beauty as expressed in the fine arts - music, art, drama and dance - and in the appreciation of colour and form. Insensitivity to aesthetic values cannot only lead to ineffective advertising and package design for products, it can also offend prospective customers. Aesthetics also embraces people's dress and appearance, i.e. their outward garments and adornments or accessories. Distinctive national attire, for instance, includes India's 'Dhoti and Saree', the Japanese kimono, Dutch clogs, and the Englishman's bowler hat and 'brollie'.

Social Organisation

Social organisation refers to the ways in which people relate to one another, form groups and organise their activities, teach acceptable behaviour and govern themselves. It thus comprises the social, educational and political systems of a society.

The businessman's ability to communicate depends to some extent, on the educational level of the foreign market. If the consumers are largely illiterate, advertising materials or package labels may have to be adapted to the needs of the market. In this regard, however, a company marketing baby food in a certain African country put the picture of a smiling child on the outside of the jar. The local resident assuming there were preserved babies inside, avoided the product! In addition, there are unspoken signals which identify cultural differences, from certain taboos to less obvious practices like the time taken to answer a letter. In some societies, for instance, an important issue is dealt with immediately; in others, promptness is taken as a sign that the matter is regarded as unimportant, the time taken in corresponding with the gravity of the issue.

In a culture where great importance is attached to the family unit, promotional efforts should be directed at the family rather than the individual. The size of the family unit differs from one culture to another. It can range from the nuclear family, i.e. mother, father, and children, to the extended family which includes many relatives and whose role is to provide protection, support and economic security to its members. In the extended family, characteristic of developing countries, consumption decision-making takes place in a larger unit and purchasing power patterns may be different from those evident in western cultures.

In any society, certain occupations carry more prestige, social status and monetary reward than others. In India, for example, there is a strong reluctance amongst people with university education to perform 'menial' tasks using their hands, even answering the telephone. In many countries, including France, Italy and Singapore, financial independence is considered essential for occupation-related prestige. In Japan, however, the majority of university-educated professionals tend to prefer working for large multinational firms than for themselves.

Social organisation is also evidenced in the operation of the class system, e.g. the Hindu caste system and the grouping of society members according to age, sex, political orientation, etc.

RELIGIOUS BELIEFS, ATTITUDES, VALUES, SPACE AND TIME

While language, material culture, aesthetics and social organisation are outward manifestations of a culture, it is the society's religious beliefs, attitudes and values that dictate the behaviour of its members.

Religious Beliefs

A religious system refers to the spiritual side of a culture or its approach to the supernatural. Western culture has been largely influenced by the Judeo-Christian traditions, while Eastern or Oriental cultures have been strongly influenced by Hinduism, Buddhism, Confucianism, and Taoism. Although very few religions influence business activities directly, the impact of religion on human value systems and decision-making is significant. Thus, religion exerts a considerable influence on people's actions and outlook on life, as well as on the products they buy. In certain parts of the world, such as Latin America, the influence of religion extends even beyond the individual or family and is manifested in a whole community's deep involvement in, and devotion to, the church.

A society's religious belief system often depends on its stage of human or economic development. Primitive tribesmen tend to be superstitious about life in general while people in technologically advanced cultures seem to have dismissed the notion of traditional religious worship and practice in favour of a more scientific approach to life and death.

To disregard the significance of religious beliefs or superstitions evident in a potential export market could result in expensive mistakes.

Attitudes

Attitudes are psychological states that predispose people to behave in certain ways. Attitudes may relate, for example, to work, wealth, achievement, change, the role of women in the economy, etc.

Western cultures, for example, value individualism and promote the importance of autonomy and personal achievement needs. In contrast, in many eastern and developing countries, there is a strong sense of collectivism and the importance of social and security needs. For instance, Hindu religion imparts a type of work ethics that considers work central to one's life but maintains that it must be performed as a service to others, not for one's own personal achievement.

Stereotypes are sets of attitudes in which one attributes qualities or characteristics to a person on the basis of the group to which that person belongs. An international business person's tendency to judge others by his or her personal and cultural standards instead of attempting to understand others in the context of their unique historical, political, economic and social backgrounds could, be termed an undesirable attitude.

Values

Values are judgements regarding what is valuable or important in life, and they vary greatly from one culture to another. People who are operating at a survival level will value food, shelter and clothing. Those with high security needs, on the other hand, may value job security, status, money, etc. From its value system, a culture sets norms, i.e. acceptable standards of behaviour.

Space

The concept of space is different wherever one goes. In western corporate culture, the size and location of an executive's office is usually determined by his level of seniority in the company. The locality and size of an Arab business executive's office, on the other hand, are a poor indication of the person's importance.

Conversation distance between two people is learned early in life - almost completely unconsciously. A western business executive, conditioned to operating within a certain amount of personal space, may feel uncomfortable or alarmed at the closeness and physical contact displayed in India, Middle East or Latin America, for example.

Time

Time also has a different meaning in each country. Western cultures tend to perceive time in terms of past, present and future. They are orientated towards the future and in the process of preparing for it, they save, waste, make up or spend time.

In India, giving a person a deadline is a way of indicating the degree of urgency or relative importance of the work. In the Middle East, however, time does not usually include schedules and timetables. The time required to get something accomplished depends on the relationship. With Indians the more important an event is, the earlier it is planned, which is why last minute invitations are often regarded as an insult. In planning future events with Arab business persons, it is often advisable to keep the lead time to a week or less, because other factors may intervene and take precedence.

Some time ago, an American lost a major contract in Greece because he did not appreciate the Greek concept of time. The Greek executive could not understand the American's insistence on setting time limits on the length of their business meetings - he and his colleagues were prepared to spend as much time in discussion as they felt was necessary. The American also insisted that the senior managers involved in the transaction be responsible only for working out the general principles of the deal, with the actual details being left to subordinates. Suspicious that this represented a lack of commitment on the part of the American, the Greek called off the deal.

Many factors continuously produce cultural changes in a society - new technology, population shifts, availability of scarce resources and changing values regarding the role of education or women. Culture is thus dynamic, and exporters, particularly those involved in international travel and marketing, need to regularly assess what new products and service needs have been created, who the potential buyers and users are, and how best to reach them.

(4) Technological Environment

Technological environment is the most important factor which affects the business enterprise. The faster changes in technology create problems for business enterprise. Products have shorter life span than the past because of rapid technological developments. Technology provides various advantages. Success in many industries depends on innovation and research. To promote innovation and research some companies establish research and development departments in their enterprises. For example, Japanese industries have achieved a great success because of innovation and rapid technological upgradation.

Technological environment includes the methods, techniques and approaches adopted for production of goods and services and its distribution. The varying technological environments of different countries affect the designing of products. For example, in USA and many other countries electrical appliances are designed for 110 volts. But when these are made for India, they have to be of 220 volts. In the modern competitive age, the pace of technological changes is very fast. Hence, in order to survive and grow in the market, a business has to adopt the technological changes from time to time. It may be noted that scientific research for improvement and innovation in products and services is a regular activity in most of the big industrial organizations. Nowadays, in fact, no firm can afford to persist with the outdated technologies.

Technology can be defined as the method or technique for converting inputs to outputs in accomplishing a specific task. Thus, the terms 'method' and 'technique' refer not only to the knowledge but also to the skills and the means for accomplishing a task. Technological innovation, then, refers to the increase in knowledge, the improvement in skills, or the discovery of a new or improved means that extends people's ability to achieve a given task.

> High technology has become like a force of nature. It transforms the economy, schools, consumer habits, the very character of modern life. Investors pour money into it; parents urge their children to study it; communities vie to attract its factories; decorators adopt it as a style; politicians push it as a panacea.
>
> **(Source : Science Digest Magazine)**

Technology can be classified in several ways. For example, blueprints, machinery, equipment and other capital goods are sometimes referred to as hard technology while soft technology includes management know-how, finance, marketing and administrative techniques. When a relatively primitive technology is used in the production process, the technology is usually referred to as labour-intensive. A highly advanced technology, on the other hand, is generally termed capital-intensive.

Changes in the technological environment have had some of the most dramatic effects on business. A company may be thoroughly committed to a particular type of technology, and may have made major investments in equipment and training only to see a new, more innovative and cost-effective technology emerge.

Indeed, the managing director of a multinational organisation manufacturing heavy machinery once said that the hardest part of his job had nothing to do with unions, pay or products, but with whether or not to spend money on the latest technologically improved equipment.

Computer technology has had an enormous impact on education and health care, to name but two areas affected. The advancements in medical technology, for example, have contributed to longevity in many societies. In addition, the introduction of robots in many factories has reduced the need for labour, and the use of VCR's and microcomputers has become commonplace in many homes and businesses.

Unfortunately, there is a negative side to technological progress. The introduction of nuclear weapons, for example, has made the destruction of the human race a frightening possibility. In addition, factories using modern technologies have polluted both air and water and contributed to various environmental and health-related problems.

Technology is a critical factor in economic development. Because of the advances of international communication, the increasing economic interdependence of nations, and the serious scarcity of vital natural resources, the transfer of technology has become an important preoccupation of both industrialised and developing countries. For many industrialised countries, the changes in the technological environment over the last 30 years have been immense particularly in such areas as chemicals, drugs, and electronics. It is vital that organisations stay abreast of these changes - not only because this will allow them to incorporate new and innovative designs into their products, but also because it will give them a firmer base from which to anticipate and counteract competition from other organisations.

When the Gillette company developed a superior stainless steel razor blade, it feared that such a superior product might mean fewer replacements and sales. Thus, the company decided not to market it. Instead, Gillette sold the technology to Wilkinson, a British garden tool manufacturer, thinking that Wilkinson would use the technology only in the production of garden tools. When Wilkinson Sword Blades were introduced and sold quickly, Gillette understood the magnitude of its mistake.

The transfer of technology is essential for attaining a high level of industrial capability and competitiveness. Multinational corporations are playing an increasingly important role in technology transfer because they invest abroad to expand production, marketing and research activities. There is also a growing consciousness amongst governments of the need to increase technology transfer to the developing countries to help stabilise their economic and social conditions.

In spite of the many differences in social, political, cultural, geographic and economic conditions, there are some common characteristics in the technological environments of developing countries. The most common technology transfer from industrialised to developing countries has been in agriculture and health care. As a result of improved health care systems, infant mortality rates have been cut while the incidence of once common diseases such as malaria and typhoid has been reduced in India, Latin America, south-east Asia and Africa. Similarly, agricultural technology has increased agricultural productivity in India, Brazil and elsewhere. However, in most developing countries, technology has made little impact on the productive systems, income distribution and living conditions of the majority of the population.

Technology transfer is a complex, time-consuming and costly process, and the successful implementation of such a process demands continuous communication and co-operation between the parties involved. Furthermore, technology transfer cannot be effective if it experiences conflict with the economic and social needs of the recipient country. The agricultural development of north-eastern Brazil, for example, was largely financed by international banks and financial organisations in the 1960's. Much of this region had been inhabited by Brazilian aborigines but it was owned by a small number of wealthy landowners. The introduction of large-scale mechanical agricultural technology in areas of the tropical rain forest of the Amazon has caused serious environmental damage such as erosion of tropical topsoil and the destruction of the natural environment of numerous birds and animals, and has displaced a large number of the local inhabitants of the forests.

Technology transfer may become a serious source of conflict between donor and recipient countries. The recipient country may feel that the donor is trying to dominate it through technology, capital and production. Dependence on foreign technology can be viewed as a serious threat to economic independence. Countries that export technology may experience different problems. For the seller of technology, the technology transfer can result in unemployment in the home country and future loss of technological superiority. For example, Japan transferred modern steel production technology to South Korea in the early 1970's. As labour and production costs in Japan increased, the Korean steel industry began to take over a significant portion of the previously Japanese-controlled international market. Some Japanese executives are now complaining that the cost of technology transfer has been much greater than the income received through the sale of technology.

Technology can be transferred from person to person, industry to industry and government to government, although the government of any country generally plays the most important role in facilitating or impeding the transfer process. Contacts amongst students from different countries are also a means of technology transfer as are journals, books, technical and professional publications, trade magazines and product pamphlets. Furthermore, multinational corporations play an important role in technology transfer by transferring information and technology from the parent company to subsidiaries in other countries, training foreign employees, etc.

(5) Legal Environment

Legal environment refers to the set of laws and regulations which influence the business organization and their operations. Every business organization has to obey and work within the framework of law. The legal environment is derived partly from the political climate in a country and has three distinct dimensions to it:

1. The laws of the home country

2. The laws of the foreign markets
3. International law in general

Legal systems vary from country to country. You are likely to find that the legal systems in operation in the buyers' country are in many respects different from that of India.

Domestic laws govern marketing within a country, e.g. the physical attributes of a product will be influenced by laws (designed to protect consumers) relating to the purity, safety or performance of the product. Domestic laws might also constrain marketers in the areas of product packaging, marking and labelling, and contracts with agents. Most countries also have certain laws regulating advertising, e.g. India does not permit any cigarette or liquor advertising on TV.

Different legal systems

The legal systems of most of the countries can be grouped into common law and code law. Common law is generally based on precedents or past practices while a code, which is a comprehensive set of volumes having statutory force and covering virtually the whole spectrum of the country's law.

India's commercial legal system has been influenced by English law. English courts create and follow precedents just as Indian courts do. Furthermore, English cases are regularly cited as authority in our courts in situations where there is no domestic decision on the point and the particular case concerns an area of our law (such as insurance or negotiable instruments) which derives from, or was considerably influenced by English law.

Contracts

Central to all commercial activities is the contract. The purpose of a contract is to specify the respective rights and obligations of the parties to an agreement and outline specific procedures or actions that must take place. In this way, the possibility of disputes arising between the parties is reduced. Indian Contract Act (1872) applies for all domestic contractual obligations.

In many cases, a contract is entered into once the agreement has been reached. It is important to agree at the beginning of the negotiations that all agreements are reduced to writing before contracts are formalised.

When an international commercial dispute occurs, the problem must be settled in one of the countries involved according to the laws and regulations of that country unless the contract states otherwise. If the dispute cannot be settled amongst the parties involved, resolution can possibly be obtained through arbitration (i.e. through negotiations facilitated by a independent third party). Where the process of arbitration fails, for one reason or another, the option of litigation, i.e. going to court, might be considered. Disputes that go to court usually involve either large monetary transactions or the ownership of patents, copyright or physical property. Court actions can take from a few months to several years and can involve large expenditure in legal fees and lost revenues.

International Law

Buyers and sellers are at times also subject to international law, which may be defined as that body of rules which regulates relationships between countries or other international legal persons. There is neither an 'international parliament' empowered to create international law; nor an 'international police force' to enforce it.

The principal sources of international law are treaties and conventions. These are created when several countries reach agreement on a certain matter and bind themselves to it by authorising their representatives to sign a document embodying that agreement. Essentially, they have entered into a contract that obliges them to do something or to refrain from doing something. Failure to comply is the equivalent of breach of contract.

Other sources of international law are custom (i.e. international practice that is accepted as law) and the general principles of law recognised by civilised nations or natural law (the basis of human coexistence). Although there is no organised body to 'enforce' international law, there is an International Court of Justice situated at The Hague in The Netherlands. This court decides any matter which the parties regard as suitable for submission to it for adjudication. This means that a country approaches the court voluntarily; it cannot be 'brought' to the court involuntarily.

Before a country is liable to comply with the provisions of a treaty or a convention, it must have signed the original protocol (i.e. the original treaty document or minutes of the convention). Once a country has signed the protocol, the method of enforcement depends on the terms of the treaty or convention. A common way of bringing a defaulting country to heel is by imposing sanctions against it. Sanctions may take many different forms and can be applied with varying degrees of severity. Obviously, the more parties there are to the protocol, the easier it is to enforce by virtue of the weight of opinion and the efficacy of any measures that can be taken against an offender.

The Incoterms (2000), as published by the International Chamber of Commerce, are not, strictly speaking, part of international law.

There has been no treaty or convention whereby countries have bound themselves to the use and meaning of Incoterms. The Incoterms have been published merely as an aid to international trade. Some countries have incorporated the Incoterms in their domestic laws by legislation but, in most cases, they are merely a guide. However, their usage has, largely, become a norm in international trade.

Another area in which international law plays an important role is in controlling the use of the sea and the environment outside the territorial waters of countries. The control of international air travel by organisations such as IATA (International Airline Transport Association), or structures such as The Hague-Visby Rules in relation to ocean freight, may also be regarded as part of international law.

Businessmen need to be able to recognise the legal significance of their actions in the general course of marketing and export-related activities both in Indian and abroad. Potentially costly errors will be avoided and should develop greater confidence in conducting negotiations at both a domestic and international level.

The important legislations that concern the business enterprises include:

(1) Indian Contract Act, 1872
(2) The Sale of Goods Act, 1930
(3) Companies Act, 1956
(4) Foreign Exchange Management Act, 1999
(5) Factories Act, 1948
(6) Industrial Disputes Act, 1972
(7) Payment of Gratuity Act, 1972
(8) Industries (Development and Regulations) Act, 1951.
(9) Prevention of Food Adulteration Act, 1945
(10) Essential Commodities Act, 2002.
(11) The Standards of Weights and Measures Act, 1956
(12) Monopolies and Restrictive Trade Act, 1969
(13) Trade Marks Act, 1999
(14) Bureau of Indian Standards Act, 1986
(15) Consumers Protection Act
(16) Competition Act, 2002

Besides, the above legislations the following are also the part of the legal environment of business.

PROVISIONS OF THE CONSTITUTION

The provisions of the articles of the Indian Constitution, particularly directive principles, rights and duties of citizens, legislative powers of the central and state government also influence the operation of business enterprises.

The Constitution of India in Part XIII, wide Articles 301 to 305, deals with freedom of Trade, Commerce and Intercourse. Out of these articles, Article 301 creates an overall limitation on all legislative powers of the Union and the State legislature. The bar on state powers to interfere in the free trade, commerce and intercourse (Article 301) is loosened by Article 302,303 and 304. Article 305 provides for state monopoly.

Study of the Articles 302 to 305 will reveal when and how the Constitution of India permits the government to restrict freedom of trade, commerce and intercourse.

Article 301: The trade and commerce throughout the territory of India shall be free and without restriction. The restriction can generally may be way of taxes. The taxes may be compensatory where they are levied for any service provided it is not taken as restriction.

But if the tax is levied to regulate or to prevent certain people from carrying on business, it amounts to restriction.

Thus the object of Article 301 is to break down the barriers between the states and to make the country as one unit with a view to encourage trade and commerce.

Article 302: However, the Parliament can impose restrictions on freedom of trade commerce and intercourse in public interest.

Article 303: The Parliament while imposing restrictions under Article 302, cannot discriminate between different states. However, the parliament can discriminate in case of scarcity of goods.

Article 304: It enables state legislature to impose taxes on goods coming from other states, if goods produced within the state are subjected to such taxes.

Article 305: Any law passed by the Union thereby creating the state monopoly shall not be affected by the provision of Part XIII of the Constitution of India.

(6) Natural Environment

Natural environment refers to geographical and ecological factors which are beyond the control of the enterprise. It include natural resources, weather and climatic conditions, landforms, rainfall, environmental pollution, etc. Climate and weather conditions affect the location of certain industries like textile industries. Similarly, environmental pollution in the form of air pollution, water pollution, and noise pollution have caused disturbances in ecological balance. Government has framed various acts for the control of environmental pollution. The business enterprise must keep in mind these factors. The natural environment includes geographical and ecological factors that influence the business operations. These factors include the availability of natural resources, climatic conditions, location aspect, topographical factors, etc. Business is greatly influenced by the nature of natural resources or environment. For example, sugar factories are set up only at those places where sugarcane is grown. It is always considered better to establish manufacturing unit near the sources of input. Further, government policies to maintain ecological balance, conservation of natural resources, etc. put additional responsibility on the business sector.

(7) **Demographical Environment**

This refers to the size, density, distribution and growth rate of population. All these factors have a direct bearing on the demand for various goods and services. For example, a country where population rate is high and children constitute a large section of population, there is more demand for baby products. Similarly, its demands of the people of cities and towns are different than the people of rural areas. The high rise of population indicates the easy availability of labour. These encourage the business enterprise to use labour-intensive techniques of production. Moreover, availability of stated labour in certain areas motivates the firms to set up their units in such areas. For example, the business units from America, Canada, Australia, Germany, U.K. are coming to India due to easy availability of skilled manpower. Thus a firm that keeps a watch on the change in the demographic front and reads them accurately will find opportunities knocking at its door steps. Demographic environment affects the business externally. Demographic environment differs from country to country and from place to place within the same country. Demographic factors includes size of population growth, family size, age composition, sex composition, urban-rural population education level, etc. Huge population size indicates cheap labour and more demand for goods and services. If population size is large then, there will be more demand for goods and services. It will have favourable impact on business. Similarly, education level is also an important demographic factor affecting business. If public is highly educated, supply of unskilled labour will decrease. On the other hand if education level is low then supply of unskilled labour will increase.

(8) International Environment

International environment is an important component of the business environment. International environment affects the business differently. International environment is very important for certain types of business. It is particularly important for industries directly depending on imports on exports. Liberalization of imports may help some industries but may adversely affect other industries. For example, the entry of multinational such as LG, Samsung in electronics industry has adversely affected the market share of domestic business firms.

QUESTION BANK

SECTION-A (Two Marks Questions)

1. Define business environment.
2. Define external environment.
3. Define internal environment.
4. Define micro-environment.
5. Define macro-environment.
6. What is economic environment of business?
7. What is political environment of business?
8. What is socio-cultural environment of business?
9. What is technological environment of business?
10. What is legal environment of business?

SECTION-B (Analytical/Descriptive Questions)

1. Briefly discuss the meaning and importance of business environment.
2. Bring out the components of business environment.
3. Write a note on external environment of business.
4. Write a note on internal environment of business.
5. Bring out the importance of macro-environment of business.
6. Bring out the importance of micro-environment of business.
7. Analyse the importance of economic environment of business.
8. Discuss the importance of political environment of business.
9. Write a note on the importance of socio-cultural environment of business.
10. Discuss the importance of legal environment of business.

SECTION-C (Essay Type Questions)

1. Explain the nature of business environment. Elucidate your answer.
2. Differentiate between micro- and macro-environment of business.
3. Bring out the importance of socio-cultural environment of business and how does it influence the business.
4. Differentiate between internal and external environment of business.
5. 'Business is an economic activity'. Explain this with the help of illustrations.
6. Explain the statement 'A business firm is an economic unit'. Give examples.
7. 'Is business decision-making an economic process'? Substantiate your answer.
8. Political environment in a country is vital for progress in business. Elaborate your answer with examples.
9. Explain few economic indicators one should consider while doing business in a country.
10. What is the importance of natural environment in business activities?

Unit 5

Government and Business

Meaning and Importance – Impact of Government policy on business and industry with reference to liberalization – Privatization and globalization.

LEARNING OBJECTIVES

This chapter takes the reader to understand the role of government and business. It assists the reader to understand various positive and negative issues associated with government under post-liberalized and globalized environment. It tries to ignite some creative ideas to compete successfully in the global environment.

5

Government and Business

MEANING AND IMPORTANCE OF GOVERNMENT

Government refers to the legislation, administration and arbitrators in the administrations bureaucracy who control a state at a given time, and to the system of government by which they are organized.

Government is the means by which state policy is enforced, as well as the mechanism for determining the policy of the state. A form of governance or form of state governance refers to the set of political institutions by which a government of state is organized.

States are served by a continuous succession of different governments. Each successive government is composed of a body of individuals who control and exercise control over political decision-making. Their function is to make and enforce laws and arbitrate conflicts. In democracy type, the political rules remain, but there is a frequent turnover of the people actually filling the positions.

The word government derives from the Latin infinitive gubre-mon, meaning "to govern" or "to manage". In parliamentary system, the word "government" is used to refer to what in presidential systems would be the executive branch and to governing party. In parliamentary system, the government is composed of the Prime Minister and the Cabinet.

The Purpose of Government

The purpose of government is to provide a system in which individuals give their portions of their freedom in order to pursue needs and wants without fears that are inherit in a state of.

Therefore, at its most basic level, the purpose of government is to protect the people from threats, both within and outside. Therefore, the fundamental purpose of government is the maintenance of basic security and public order without which individuals cannot find happiness.

The only purpose of government is to protect man's rights, which means to protect him from physical violence.

A proper government is like a policeman, acting as an agent of man's self-defense and such that may resort to force only against those who start the use of force.

The functions of government are:

(1) The police – to protect from criminals.
(2) The army – to protect from foreign invaders.
(3) The courts – to protect property and contracts from breach or fraud by others.

The very purpose of the government is to protect the individual rights of its citizens. Since rights can be assaulted both within a country or outside of it, the government must deal with both. This requires an army or defence of the country, and a police system to protect the individual citizen from other individuals within the country. The government requires a legal system, where laws are enforced to protect the interest of the citizen.

Imagine for a moment if there was no government, prevailing in the country, what would be the world around like. That is a pretty sufficient reason to give the importance of government in a country:

(1) Man is a social animal for a society to stabilize and grow in peace, it is necessary that man becomes a political animal, and adopt a particular type of government.
(2) A government is any organization that holds the highest power in a region or a country and is ultimate in matters of public policy, law and order. A nation state is defined by the existence of a government which has control over a nation's dominion. The three branches of government include:
    (a) the executive
    (b) the legislative
    (c) the judicial

    These are the three pillars on which the edifice of a democratic government exists.
(3) There can be various governments depending on how power in a region or a country is shared among the people.
(4) The government is guided by a chosen set of principles which are together assimilated into a constitution. Most decisions are made by a central government which is made up of a set of elected representatives.

Purpose and Importance of Government

(1) *Upholding fundamental rights:* The prime importance of government is to uphold and protect the fundamental human rights of freedom, equality, peace, justice. Most importantly, must be safeguarded is freedom of thought, freedom to determine the destiny, and above all the right to pursuit happiness.

(2) *Maintaining peace through enforcement of law and order:* To maintain peace the government needs to enforce law and maintain order. It needs to establish an impartial judicial system that can deliver justice and punish crime. A creation of an initial organization for implementing the rule of law must be established. This function includes the safeguarding the property and life of citizens.

(3) *Protecting the sovereignty of the nation:* Another prime purpose in importance of the government is to create laws safeguarding land and people from elements that threaten the nation. For this, defense forces protect its borders and its economic intents. This is important one of the most purposes of government.

(4) *Implementing economic and social reforms:* Another prime purpose of a government, is to create laws that achieve economic as well as social reform. The policies of the government must be repaired or modified according to the need. This is done by electing the representatives of the people.

(5) *Collecting taxes:* The economic resources of the government, gives the provision of a all governance facilities and implementation of policies cannot be possible without collection of taxes from the general public. It needs to have an impartial taxation system for the purpose.

(6) *Providing education, infrastructure, health facilities:* The most fundamental of human needs which include education, food, health facilities are taken care of through policies of the government. Government provides infrastructure like roads, building, hospitals, etc., where those needs are met.

Government of India

The government of India officially known as the Union Government was established by the Constitution of India, and the governing authority of the union of 28 states and seven territories, collectively called the Republic of India. It is seated in Delhi, the capital of India.

The Government comprises three branches:
(1) The executive
(2) The legislative
(3) The judiciary

(1) The executive branch is headed by the president, who is the head of state and exercises his or her power directly or through officers subordinate to him.
(2) The legislative branch or parliament consists of the lower house, the Lok Sabha, and the Upper House the Rajya Sabha as well as the president.
(3) The Judicial branch has the Supreme Court at its apex, 21 High Courts and numerous civil, criminal, and family courts at district level.

India is the largest democracy in the world.

The legislature is the parliament. It is bicameral consisting of two houses:

(i) The directly elected 545 member Lok Sabha – "The House of people" – Lower House
(ii) Indirectly elected 250 member and appointed Rajya Sabha "Council of States" – The Upper House.

Parliament enjoys parliamentary supremacy. All the members of the council of minister as well as the Prime Minister are members of the Parliament. If they are not, they must be elected within a period of six months from the time they assume their respective office. The Prime Minister and its council of ministers are responsible for Lok Sabha collectively.

The executive power is vested in mainly the President of India by article 53(1) of the constitution. The President enjoys all constitutional powers and exercises them directly or through officers subordinate to him as per the aforesaid Article 53(1).

The President is to act in accordance with aid and advice tendered by the head of Government (Prime Minister of India) and his or her Council of Ministers (the Cabinet) as described in Article 74 (Constitution of India). The constitution vests in the President of India all the executive powers of the Central Government. The President appoints the Primer Minster, the person most likely to command the support of the majority in the Lok Sabha (usually the leader of the majority party on coalition). The President then appoints the other members of the Council of Ministers distributing portfolios to them on the advice of the Prime Minister.

The council of ministers remains in power during the 'pleasure' of President. In practice, however, the council of ministers must retain the support of the Lok Sabha. If it President were to dismiss the Council of Minister on his/her initiative it might trigger a constitutional crisis, the Council of Ministers be discussed as long as it commands the support of a majority in the Lok Sabha.

The Vice-President of India is the second highest government official in the executive branch of the Government of India after the President. The Vice-President also has the legislative function of acting as the Chairman of the Rajya Sabha.

The Vice-President acts as a President in the event of death, resignation or removal of President until a new President is chosen by the electoral committee for maximum of 6 months. During this period the Vice-President shall not perform the duties of the office of the Chairman of Rajya Sabha.

Impact of Government Policy on Business and Industry

Economic reforms/environment affects the business and industry directly. Business plans and programmers are directly influenced by economic factors, such as interest rates, money supply, price level consumers credit, etc. Economic conditions leading to inflation or deflation affect the business activities. Inflation leads to rise in general price-levels whereas deflation leads to fall in price level. Higher petrol prices in the country related a trend in favour of small cars like Maruti car. State of industrial trade and business booms and slumps constitute the economics of market environment.

Recently government had initiated various economic policies. As such these influence business and industry in the following manner:

(1) buyer's market
(2) export is required for survival
(3) corporate vulnerability
(4) threat from multinational companies
(5) overall competition
(6) world class technology
(7) future not guided by past failures.

(1) Buyer's Market

In the liberalized policy regime shortage of goods is no more, but there are surplus of goods. This arises due to competition, reduction in cost upgradation of technology, improvements in quality and customer convenience. Removal of government restrictions on capacity creation and capacity utilization has also helped increase in supply of goods. Industry has been given total freedom to expand. Price control has been removed. Investments now takes place in the areas of demand. All these changes have been made the buyer, the sovereign of the market.

(2) Export is Required for the Survival

Implementation of new trade policy has linked imports to exports. The enterprise should fetch foreign exchange by exports and use of the same for importing raw materials, spares and equipment, etc. For example, Reliance Group, Essar World Trade, Ceat, Videocon, Eicher, MRF, etc., are benefited by the new government policy.

(3) Corporate Vulnerability

Due to pressure from multinationals, Indian companies are facing takeovers, subordinate position in joint ventures, unequal battle among the competitors and financial weakness. For instances DCM Daewoo had to pour only 6 crore as investment in the joint venture, whereas Daewoo pumped 468 crore equity which is about 92% of the total investment.

(4) Threat from Multinational Companies

Due to the present policy of liberalization of our government, massive entry of multinationals in the country has started. The vast resources and the modern technology of the present multinational companies have enabled their subsidiary Indian companies boost sales and enjoy strategic advantage over their competitors. The presence of multinational companies has been rendering valuable services to our economy. It is supplying superior quality of goods, generating more employment opportunities, promoting modern technology and awakening our business community.

(5) Overall Competition

The new competitive environment has thrown the economy open. There is tough competition between multinationals and there is also competition between Indian enterprises and foreign enterprises. Completion has now become global. It is not confined to national boundaries. For instance, Weston Electronic Company which held about 18% of the television market has been virtually thrown out of the market due to cut-throat competition and technological backwardness.

(6) World Class Technology

Changes in government policy regarding business and industry has provided us with world class technology. Indian companies have also started making investment in research and development. Pharmaceutical industries made 2-1 investment in R&D. In developed countries investment in research and development goes about 12%. Multinationals are also bringing world class technology in the country. This has enabled faster growth of industries.

(7) Future not guided by Past Failures

It is rightly said that future starts afresh for Indian companies. Future, now needs new strategies, higher technologies, determined efforts, enthusiasm, organization and leadership. New approaches, systems structures and new leadership must emerge to compete with the multinationals. We must forget the past, bury its failures and start working with new endeavour, approaches and leadership. Government policies have a major impact on the competitiveness and profitability of industries. It has got three major contributions—first it helps direct attention to those policies which have the serious effect on performance of an industry. Second, it recognises both positive and negative effect of policy measures an industry. Third, it shows that the policies can have important spillover effects when industries are linked vertically through markets.

Government creates rules and regulations in which businesses are able to compete against each other. From time to time the government will change these rules and frameworks forcing business to change the way they operate. Business is then keenly affected by government policies. Other areas of government policies that affect business are:

(1) economic policy
(2) competitive business environment
(3) taxation policy
(4) interest rates
(5) government spending policy
(6) legal changes
(7) exchange rates
(8) public–private partnership
(9) political culture

(1) Economic Policy

A key area of government economic policy is the role that the government gives to the state in the economy. Between 1945 and 1979 the government increasingly interfered in the economy by creating state run industries which usually took the form of public corporations. However, from 1979 onwards we saw industries were sold off to private shareholders.

(2) Competitive Business Environment

With the introduction of privatization the industries have become more competitive wherein which industries were sold off to private shareholders to create a more competitive business environment.

(3) Taxation Policy

Taxation policy affects business costs. For example, a rise in corporation tax (on business profits) has the same effect as increase in costs. Business can pass some of this tax on to consumers in higher prices, but it will also affect the bottom lines. Other business taxes are environment taxes (e.g., landfill tax) and VAT (Value Added Tax). VAT is actually passed down the line to the final consumer but the administration of the VAT system is a cost for business. High tax rate on imported goods would encourage local entrepreneurs to produce goods at home.

(4) Interest Rate

In this country the level of interest rate is determined by a government appointed group—the Monetary Policy Committee which meets every month. A rise in interest rates increases the costs to business of borrowing money, and also causes consumers to reduce expenditure.

(5) Government Spending Policy

Government spending policy also affects business. For example, if the government spends more on schools, this will increase the income of business that supply schools with books, equipment, etc. Government also provides subsidies for some business activity, e.g., an employment subsidy take on the long-term unemployed people.

(6) Legal Changes

The government regularly changes laws in line with its political policies. As a result businesses have to respond to changes in the legal framework. Examples of changes of legal changes include:

(i) The creation of a national minimum wage which has recently been extended.

(ii) The requirement for business to cater for disabled people by building ramps into offices, shops, etc.

(iii) Providing increasingly tight protection for consumers to protect them against unscrupulous business practice.

(iv) Creating rules on what constitutes fair competition between businesses.

(7) Exchange Rate

The government policies of a country have high bearing on exchange rates. The economy of the country always depends on GDP growth in the national as well as international markets. So, if the GDP fluctuates in the market it will have serious impact on the exchange rates. So, with decrease or increase of exchanges rate will impact severely industry or business growth as a whole.

The policy of export and import (Exim policy) also has a serious impact or exchange rate fluctuations.

(8) Public-Private Partnership

Public and private partnership also plays a very important role on business and industry. The public-private partnership must have strong strategic planning, and the planning should be strategically implemented in the market, where the companies are playing in both national as well as international markets. So, the image of the company makes an impact on the fluctuations of exchange rates, interest rates, etc., in the national as well as international markets.

(9) Political Culture

The government policy of a country depends upon its political culture. It can also vary depending on the form of government. The government policy in a politically stable country will be different from unstable country. In a stable political system, the government can take sustained business-friendly decisions to strengthen the local business. The government in this situation, gets the help of opposition. But in an unstable political system in which the opposition boycotts parliament and takes to street agitations business and investment would suffer. In such a negative political culture, a country cannot have a sustained business-friendly environment on policy. In an unstable system, a government finds it difficult to maintain law and order which affects the business environment. It hampers business. Foreign investors do not invest in such an environment.

LIBERALISATION, PRIVATISATION, GLOBALISATION

Recent Developments in Indian Economy

The economic environment of business in India, has been changing at a faster rate mainly due to the changes in the economic policies of the government. At the time of independence, the Indian economy was basically agrarian with a weak industrial base. To speed up the industrial growth and solve various economic problems, the government took several steps like state ownership on certain categories of industries, economic planning, reduced role of private sector, etc. The government adopted several control measures on the functioning of private sector enterprises. All these efforts resulted in a mixed response. There was growth in net national product, per capital income and developments of capital goods sector and infrastructure. But the rate of industrial growth was slow, inflation increased and the government faced a serious foreign exchange crisis during eighties. As a result, the Government of India introduced a radical change in economic policies in 1991. This policy abolished industrial licensing in most of the cases and allowed private participation in most industries. Disinvestment was carried out in many public sector industrial enterprises and opened up the economy considerably. Foreign Investments Promotion Board was set up to channelise foreign capital investment in India. Let us discuss the development under three heads, viz., (a) Liberalisation, (b) Privatisation, (c) Globalisation.

(a) Liberalisation

Liberalisation refers to the process of eliminating unnecessary controls and restrictions on the smooth functioning of business enterprises. It includes:

(i) Abolishing industrial licensing requirements in most of the industries.
(ii) Freedom in deciding the scale of business activities.
(iii) Freedom in fixing prices of goods and services.
(iv) Simplifying the procedure for imports and exports.
(v) Reduction in tax rates.
(vi) Simplified policies to attract foreign capital and technology to India.

Through this liberalization process, "Indian economy has opened up and started interaction with the world in a big way. This has resulted in easy entry of foreign business organizations in India. This has further resulted in stiff competition and efficiency. Ultimately, liberalization has helped us in achieving a high growth rate, easy availability of goods at competitive rates, a healthy and flourishing stock market, high foreign exchange reserve, low inflation rate, strong super values, good industrial relations, etc.

It was in the 1991 that first steps towards globalisation and economic liberalisation were undertaken by Dr. Manmohan Singh, who was the Finance Minister of India under the Congress government headed by P.V. Narasimha Rao. This is perhaps the milestone in the economic growth of India and it aimed towards welcoming globalisation. Economic condition of the country gradually started improving and today India is one of the fastest growing economies in the world with an average of yearly growth rate of around 66.7%.

(b) Privatisation

Privatisation refers to reducing the role of public sector by involving the private sector in most activities. Due to the policy reforms announced in 1991, the expansion of public sector has laterally come to half and the private sector registered fast growth in the post-liberalized period. The issues of privatization include:

(i) Reduction in the number of industries reserved for the public sector from 17 to 8 (reduced further to 3 later on) and the introduction of selective competition in the reserved area.

(ii) Disinvestment of shares of selected public sector industrial enterprises in order to raise resources and to encourage wider participation of general public and workers in the ownership in business.

(iii) Improvement in performance through an MOU system by which managements are to be granted greater autonomy but held accountable for specified results.

In India as a result of these steps, the post-liberalization phase, has witnessed a massive expansion of the private sector business in India. You can have an idea of their expansion from the fact that the total capital employed in top 500 private sector companies rose from Rs. 1,39,806 crore in 1992-93 to Rs. 2,34,751 crore in 1994-95 (an expansion of 681 in just two years).

Important reasons for privatisation in India are:

The first order issue is that of competition policy. When the government hinders competition by blocking entry or FDI, this is damaging. Once competitive conditions are ensured, there are indeed, benefits from shifting labour and capital to more efficient hands through privatisation, but this is a second order issue. The reasons are:

(1) Releasing the large amount of public resources locked up in non-strategic PSEs for redeployment in the areas that are much higher on the social priority, such as, basic health, family welfare, primary education and social and essential infrastructure.

(2) Stemming further outflow of these scarce public resources sustaining the unviable non-strategic PSE.

(3) Reducing the public dept that is threatening to assume unmanageable proportions.

(4) Transferring the commercial risk to which the taxpayer's money locked up in the public sector, is exposed, to the private sector wherever the private sector is willing and able to step in.

(5) Releasing other tangible and intangible resources, such as, large manpower currently locked up in managing the PSEs and their

time and energy, for redeployment in high priority social sectors which are short of sector resources.

The need for privatisation arises out of the situations like:

(1) Control of budgeting deficit
(2) Resource mobilisation
(3) Reduction of extra tax burden
(4) Flow of funds to public
(5) Production increase
(6) Retrieval of civil servants from public enterprises to better utilisation in governance and administration.
(7) Increase in competition, both in domestic as well as international markets.

Based on the recommendations of the Arjun Sen Gupta Committee on public sector enterprise, the privatisation of public enterprises in India can take one of the following form:

(1) Complete privatisation
(2) Partial privatisation
(3) Privatisation of the management
(4) Creating competitive conditions
(5) Deregulation
(6) Delicenesing
(7) Disinvestment and other liberalisation measures.

As a consequence they must also follow the trend of the overall economic policy. Which in the current control, is heavily tilted towards liberalisation, democratisation, marketisation, and globalisation and a decesive move away from extensive social controls.

(c) Globalisation

Globalisation may be defined as "the growing economic interdependence of countries worldwide through increasing volume and variety of cross-border transactions in goods and services and of international capital flows, and also through the more rapid and widespread diffusion of technology. Globalisation is unstoppable so the challenge is how to live with it and take advantage of the opportunities.

In simple words, globalisation means, 'integrating' the economy of a country with the world economy. This implies free flow of goods and services, capital, technology and labour across national boundaries. To achieve these objectives of globalisation, the government has adopted various measures such as reduction in custom duties, removal of quantitative restrictions or quotas or exports and imports, facilitating foreign investments and encouragement of foreign technology. These measures are expected to achieve a higher rate of growth, enlargements of employment potential, and reduction of regional disparities.

Globalisation is the new catch phrase in the world economy, dominating the world since the nineties of the last century. People relied more on the market economy, had more faith in private capital and resources, international organisations started playing a vital role in the development of developing countries. The impact of globalisation has been fair enough on the developing economies to a certain extent. It brought along with it varied opportunities for the developing countries. It gave a better access to the developed markets. The technology transfer promised better productivity and thus improved standard of living.

Globalisation may be considered at two levels, viz., at the macro-level (i.e., globalisation of the world economy) and at the micro-level (i.e., globalisation of the business and the firms). Globalisation of the world economy is achieved, quite obviously, by globalizing the national economies. Globalisation of the economics and globalization of business are inter-dependent.

Economic integration by 'globalisation' enabled the cross-country free flow of information, ideas, technologies, goods, services, capital, finance, and people. This cross-border integration had different dimensions cultural, social, political and economic. More or less the economic integration happened through 4 channels:

(1) trade in goods and services
(2) movement of capital
(3) flow of finance
(4) movement of people

Advantages of Globalisation

The gains from globalisation can be called or cited in the context of economic globalisation.

- **Trade in Goods and Services**
  From the theoretical aspect, international trade ensures allocating different resources and that has to be consistent. This specialisation in the processes leads to better productivity. We all know from the economic perspective that restrictive trade barriers in emerging economics only impede growth. Emerging economics can reap the benefits of international trade if only all the resources are utilised in full potential. This is where the importance of reducing the tariffs and non-tariff barriers crop up.

- **Movement of Capital**

  The production base of a developing economy gets enhanced due to capital flow across countries. It was very much true in the 19th and 20th centuries. The mobility of capital only enabled savings far the entire world and exhibited high investment potential. A country's economic growth doesn't, however, get barred by domestic savings. Foreign capital inflow does play an important role in the development of an economy. To be specific, capital flows either can take the form of foreign direct investment because portfolio investment doesn't have a direct impact on the productive capacity expansion.
- **Financial Flows**

  The capital market development is one of the major features of the process of globalisation. We all know that the growth in the capital and mobility of the foreign exchange markets enabled better transfer of resources cross-borders and by large the global foreign exchange markets improved. It is mandatory to go in for the expansion of foreign exchange markets and thus facilitate international transfer of capital. The major example of such international transfer of funds led to the financial criseis – which has by now become a worrying phenomenon.
- **Movement of People**

  Apart from the low cost of labour, there are several other aspects of human resources to Indian favour. India has one of the largest pool of scientific and technical manpower. The number of management graduates is also surging. It is widely recognised that given the right environment, Indian scientists and technical personnel can do excellently. Similarly, the labour productivity in India is generally low, given the right environment it will be good. While several countries are facing labour shortage and may face diminishing labour supply, India presents the opposite picture. Cheap labour has particular attraction for several industries. The led the outsourcing industry in boom in India. This shows the movement of people across borders for job across the world.
- **Wide Base**

  India has a very broad resource and industrial base which can support a wide variety of business.
- **Growing Entrepreneurship**

  Many of the established industries are planning to go international in a big way. Added to this considerable growth of new and dynamic entrepreneurs who could make a significant contribution to the globalisation of Indian business.

- **Growing Domestic Market**
  The growing domestic market enables the Indian companies to consolidate their position and to gain more strength to make foray into the foreign market or to expend their foreign business. The growing population and disposable increase and the resultant expanding market provides entrances business opportunities in the global market.
- **Competition**
  The growing competition, both from internal and external, provokes many Indian companies to look into foreign markets seriously to improve their competitive position and to increase the business. Sometimes companies enter foreign market as a counter-competitive strategy, i.e., to fight the foreign company in its own home market to weaker its competitive strength. So, there also have a breathy competition across the world.

Disadvantages of Globalisation

The Indian business suffers from a number of disadvantages in respect of globalisation of business. The important problems are the following:

(1) Government Policy and Procedure
Government policy and procedures in India are among the most complex, confusing and cumbersome in the world. Even after the much publicised liberalisation they do not present a very conducive situation. One prerequisite for success in globalisation is swift and efficient action. Government policy and the bureaucratic culture in India in this respect are not that encouraging.

(2) High Cost
High cost of many vital inputs and other is generally other factors like raw materials and intermediaries, power, finance, infrastructural facilities like port, etc., tend to reduce the international competitiveness of the Indian business.

(3) Poor Infrastructure
Infrastructure in the country is generally inadequate and inefficient and therefore, very costly. This is a serious problem affecting the growth as well as competitiveness.

(4) Obsolescence
The technology employed, modes and style of operation, etc., in generally, obsolete and these seriously affect the competitiveness.

(5) Resistance to Changes
There are several socio-political factors while resist change and this comes in the way of modernisation and efficiency improvement. Technological modernization is resisted due to fear of unemployment. The extent of excess labour employed by the

industry is alarming. Because of this labour productivity is very low and this in some cases more than affects the advantages of cheap labour.

(6) Poor Quality Image and Supply Problem

Due to various reasons the quality of many products is poor. Even when the quality is good, the poor quantity image India has become a handicap.

Due to various reasons like low production capacity, shortages of raw materials and infrastructure like power and port facilities, Indian companies in many instances are not able to accept large orders and keep up delivery schedules.

(7) Limited R&D and Marketing Research

Marketing research and R&D is other areas are vital inputs for development of international business. However, these are poor in Indian business. Expenditure on R&D is less than one per cent of GNP while it is two or three per cent in most of the developed countries.

(8) Trade Barriers

Although the tarriff barriers to trade have been progressively reduced, thanks to the GATT/WTO, the non-tarriff barriers have been increasing, particularly in the developed countries. Further, the trading blocks like the NAFTA, EC, etc., could also adversely affect India's business.

(9) Small Size and Lack of Experience

Because of the small size and the low level of resources in many cases Indian firms are not able to compete with the giants of other countries. Even the largest of the Indian companies are small compared to the multinational giants.

The general lack of experience in international business is another important problem for Indian business.

Globalisation has also thrown open varied challenges such as inequality overseas and within different nations, volatility in financial market. Another negative aspect of globalization is that the majority of third world countries stayed away from the entire lime light. Till the nineties, the process of globalisation in the Indian economy had been guarded by trade, investment, and financial barriers. Due to this, the liberalisation process took time to hasten up. The pace of globalisation did not start that smoothly.

The intent of globalisation is efficiency improvement and market optimisation taking advantages of the opportunities of the global environment. Therefore, in many cases, Indian companies have to globalise to survive and grow in the emerging competitive environment.

POINTS TO REMEMBER

Meaning of Government : A body of people that sets and administers public policy, and exercises executive, political, and sovereign power through customs, institutions, and laws within a state.

MEANING OF BUSINESS

An economic system in which goods and services are exchanged for one another or money, on the basis of their perceived worth. Every business requires some form of investment and a sufficient number of customers to whom its output can be sold at profit on a consistent basis.

Importance of government in business:

1. Upholding fundamental rights
2. Maintaining peace through enforcement of law and order:
3. Protecting the sovereignty of the nation
4. Implementing economic and social reform
5. Collecting taxes
6. Providing education, infrastructure, health facilities

Recent economic policies:

(1) buyer's market
(2) export is required for survival
(3) corporate vulnerability
(4) threat from multinational companies
(5) overall competition
(6) world class technology
(7) future not guided by past failures.

Other economic policies:

(1) economic policy
(2) competitive business environment
(3) taxation policy
(4) interest rates
(5) government spending policy
(6) legal changes
(7) exchange rates
(8) public–private partnership
(9) political culture

LIBERALISATION

Liberalization (or liberalization) refers to a relaxation of previous government restrictions, usually in areas of social or economic policy.

PRIVATISATION

Privatization is the incidence or process of transferring ownership of a business, enterprise, agency or public service from the public sector (government) to the private sector (business).

GLOBALISATION

Globalization describes an ongoing process by which regional economies, societies and cultures have become integrated through globe-spanning networks of exchange. The term is sometimes used to refer specifically to economic globalization: the integration of national economies into the international economy through trade, foreign direct investment, capital flows, migration, and the spread of technology.

Advantages of Globalization

Trade in Goods and Services
Movement of Capital
Financial Flows
Movement of People
Wide Base
Growing Entrepreneurship
Growing Domestic Market
Competition

Disadvantages of Globalization

Government Policy and Procedure
High Cost
Poor Infrastructure
Obsolescence
Resistance to Changes
Poor Quality Image and Supply Problem
Limited R&D and Marketing Research
Trade Barriers
Small Size and Lack of Experience

QUESTION BANK

Section A - 2 Marks Questions

1. What is meant by government
2. Define the term business
3. Mention any four important roles of government towards business.
4. Define the term liberalization.
5. Define the term privatisation.
6. Define the term globalization.
7. List four advantages of globalization.
8. List four disadvantages of globalization.
9. List any two economic measures of government of India.
10. List any two trade barriers of India.

Section B

Descriptive/Analytical type questions

1. Illustrate the role of government in business.
2. Business and governments are complementary to each other, Discuss.
3. Critically evaluate the recent policies of central government towards business.
4. How does liberalization contribute to the growth of the economy. Analyze?

Section C

Essay Type Questions

1. Explain the role of government in globalization.
2. Explain the merits and demerits of privatization.
3. Write a brief note on trade barriers.
4. Explain the recent economic policies of government of India.
5. Globalization is not an option, but a compulsion to India. Discuss?

Index